Be Your Own Boss

Be Your Own Boss

Terry Prone

&

Frances Stephenson

POOLBEG

A Paperback Original
First published 1991 by
Poolbeg Press Ltd
Knocksedan House,
Swords, Co Dublin, Ireland

© Terry Prone & Frances Stephenson 1991

ISBN 1 85371 101 2

Cover design by Pomphrey Associates
Set by Richard Parfrey
Printed by Guernsey Press Vale Guernsey Channel Islands

*To a very patient John and the
chocolate-chip lady*

Acknowledgements

This book has two authors' names on it. It might just as well have had a dozen or more names—because people on whose door we knocked seeking basic information became collaborators, helpers, error-finders who helped shape the book.

We are particularly grateful to Kieran McGowan, Managing Director of the Industrial Development Authority, who gave generously of his own time and immeasurable expertise.

Desmond Fahey, Chief Executive, Dublin Business Innovation Centre, Denis Rohan of FÁS, Norman Newcombe, Group Marketing Manager of An Post, Professor Jim Ward of UCG, Pam Kearney, Senior Tax Partner of O'Hare Barry: all went to considerable trouble to make their advice relevant and understandable to laypeople.

Jane Williams, Managing Director, Commencements Ltd, Carmen Chesneau, Company Director, Baltino Ltd, Linda Cullen, Managing Diresctor, Video Unlimited, Michael O'Kelly, Kelly Kitchens and Michael O'Kelly Construction, Aibhlín McCrann and Mary Boyle happily allowed us to make case-histories of their good times and their instructional bad times. So did a few other entrepreneurs, who shall be nameless because their stories (anonymously included in the book) would give their bank managers migraines and infarctions.

Individuals who helped us were Brigid Ruane, the researcher in charge of the annual Enterprise

Late Late Show, Mike Feeney and Mairead Coffey of IDA, Tony Courtney of CTT and Norman Whelan of Court Financial Services

Organisations that assisted were: BIM, Departments of Social Welfare and Labour, Eolas, Revenue Commissioners, Shannon Development Company, Údáras na Gaeltachta and Walsh Warren & Co.

Our own company, Carr Communications, overworked and interrupted us all the time, but also gave us ideas, arguments, technology, contacts and listeners off whom to bounce ideas. Mary Boyle and Gerard Kenny know how grateful we are.

For permission to quote copyright material, the authors and publishers are grateful to the following: Random House Inc: *Doing Business Boldly* by Daniel Kehrer (1990); Harper and Row Publishers Inc: *The Myth of Neurosis, Overcoming the Illness Excuse* by Dr Garth Wood (1986); and *Doublespeak* (1989) by William Lutz; Houghton Mifflin Company/ Peter Davison: *Land's Polaroid* by Peter C Wensberg (1987); Small Business Research Trust, the Open University, Milton Keynes: *The Making of Entrepreneurs* by Graham Bennock and John Stanworth (1990); Simon and Schuster: *Growing a Business* (1987) by Paul Hawken.

Contents

1

Should You Try to Become Your Own Boss?

More people are becoming their own boss these days than at any time in the past. Not so long ago, children were brought up to aim themselves at the "permanent, pensionable" job. They expected to stay there until retirement released them. They were secure, and in return for that security, they gave loyalty.

It's not like that any more. Permanent and pensionable jobs are in much smaller supply, and many of those that existed a few years ago have disappeared, leaving bruises, redundancy packages and some surprised entrepreneurs who never knew they had it in them. Expectations are different today. If you're twenty as you read these words, the overwhelming likelihood is that you will not spend your career in one organisation. On the contrary, you will probably change employers, jobs, and even careers more than once in your working life. You will almost certainly feel less loyalty to employers than did your parents or grandparents. In the past, people often branded themselves with the name of a big employer. You were "with the Bank." You were "a Corporation man." Or you came from "a Guinness family." That last didn't mean your surname matched the one on the bottle of stout; it just meant that your seed, breed and generation considered themselves lucky to earn a living under the benign paternalism of The Brewery.

Today, the favourite pipe dream is to be your own boss, own your own business, make it all on your own. Making it more than a pipe dream takes a lot of hard work. It also requires that you be honest with yourself and examine, long before you ever set up in business, precisely why you want to set up on your own. There are good reasons. There are bad reasons. Here are some of both.

I'm Fed Up Punching a Clock

You're right. Up to a point. Signing in each day reduces many people to nail-biting blobs of ritually humiliated resentment.

For some, the fact that a Failure's Book may be substituted for an Achiever's Book on the dot of half nine, or a line drawn to separate good scouts from wicked slobs, is even more annoying than the simple task of noting down at what time you arrived for work. (Talk to the generations of mothers who had no choice but to give up work because of the marriage bar: the one good thing about that bar which they often mention is that they never again had to sign in each morning.)

If the reason you hate clock punching is that you hate getting up on time, you would be well advised to stay where you are, because all you can lose in your present place of employment are brownie points, promotion or the warm approval of your boss. As your own boss, you may punch no clock, but that's because you start earlier than nine and work much later than five. As your own boss, you will quickly discover that there is always someone younger and hungrier coming up on your inside track—unless you get up early enough to block off that inside track.

I Don't Like Working for Someone Else

If this is your main reason for giving up the day job, go now and shred your letter of resignation, because it is one of the poorest reasons you could adduce for leaving your post. If you don't like the person you work for, abandoning ship shouldn't happen until you have analysed the reasons for the dislike.

My Boss Is One of Life's Natural Disasters

8.5 on the Richter Scale of human nastiness. Can't spare the time to be his (or her) own worst enemy because he (or she) is so busy being everybody else's worst enemy. Sticks pins in everybody's balloon, rains on everybody's parade, steals candies from babies and drives too close to the car in front. You think that working for this abomination has been good training for you? Has been a useful training ground in entrepreneurship? Forget it. Go work for a human being for a couple of years to retune yourself, and only after that give serious consideration to being your own boss.

You Are Not Easy to Get Along with

Remember the old story of the man who stopped his car at a petrol station about a hundred miles from the last town and a hundred miles from the next town.

"What are the people like in the town up ahead?" he asked the petrol pump attendant.

"What were they like in the town you've just come from?" asked the attendant in return.

"Horrible," said the driver. "Mean-spirited. Crooked. Always bitching behind your back."

"Well," said the petrol pump attendant, "I think *you'll* find the people in the town up ahead just the same."

Not getting along with people in a regular job may be a problem. Not getting along with people when you're running your own business may mean bankruptcy. The boss in a new company may demand a level of performance an established company never has to ask, and the penalty for non-delivery is much tougher than a reprimand or a poor review at the end of the year. To evoke that level of performance you have to be able to motivate people, and it's a tad difficult to motivate people you don't get along with.

I Don't Like Being at Everyone's Beck and Call

Later in this book, we'll be looking at the tools of the entrepreneur's trade, but here's a free preview; many if not most of those who run their own businesses have bleeps glued to their hips, have cars with cellular phones, have FAX machines in their homes (one we know has it in her bedroom) and on arrival at the pearly gates are going to say to St Peter, "Look, I'll be right with you but before we have our discussion, would you mind if I used your phone? I just need to check on messages left for me." The average normal job requires that you be at your boss's beck and call. Running your own business puts you at the beck and call of customers, suppliers, debtors, creditors, the Revenue Commissioners, the media, the bank and six million publishers of newspapers, free sheets, directories and other consumers of the world's trees, each one of whom just knows that if you put an advertisement in their publication, it would net you sales impressive enough to make Michael Smurfit look like a smalltimer.

I Don't Get Paid Enough

Old-fashioned greed is a great motivator. As is old-fashioned self esteem; a knowledge that you are worth more than is reflected in your pay packet. Most small businesses, however, go through a period of time before they break even, and considerably more time before they make a profit, so don't start from the idea that once you go out on your own you can pay yourself a fortune. In researching this book, we encountered one company which was set up by four people who had been paid, individually and severally, very well by their four previous employers. The year of set up, each of them dropped several notches in their take-home pay. One halved his income. By year three, they were all paying themselves what they had earned as employees of other people. It took another three years before they began to take home really fat pay cheques, partly because of a market turndown in year five.

I Have More to Offer Than My Current Job Demands

This is not a very good reason for setting out to be your own boss. It may not be a reflection on the company that employs you, either. Big corporate entities, particularly big state-sponsored bodies, sometimes have limited capacity to utilise the totality of someone's skills or talents, if that someone is a bit of a Renaissance man or woman. If you know you have more to offer than your job asks of you, then your own company may benefit from a great deal of dammed-up energy and a bunch of under-utilised abilities.

I'm Never Going to Get to the Top Where I Work

Let's be honest. Sometimes excellence is what makes it to the top. Just about as frequently, what makes it to the top is the yea-sayer, the clever crawler or the owner's firstborn. Occasionally, there are prejudices running around that don't look like prejudices; one highly successful entrepreneur of our acquaintance left a prestigious company because he realised that the corporate culture favoured engineers, and although he could do well within the organisation, he was unlikely, given his background in Arts and Sociology, to get to the top. In a smaller company, especially in a smaller company set up, once upon a time, by the man still running it, an employee's conduit to career progress may be corked by the simple fact that the owner is the boss and plans to live forever and retire never. If any of these scenarios looks familiar to you, then think seriously about getting out and creating your own.

I Have a Hobby Out of Which I Think I Could Make a Business

Just be aware that a hobby turning into a business has implications for you and those around you which are not always obvious. One friend of ours has a teenage son who had a knack for gerbil propagation. Give him a couple of gerbils and in a fortnight's time he would own a population explosion. The local pet shop was happy to serve as his retailer, and he was laughing all the way to the bank. Well, to be perfectly honest, to the post office, where he kept his gerbil-gotten gains. His mother, on the other hand, was climbing the walls because gerbils, en masse, have a certain ambience (not to mention whiff) to them. The entrepreneur would be off at school, and his mother would find herself sharing an establishment with thirty or forty ever-scrabbling vermin.

"Gerbils are not vermin," the entrepreneur said, crossly.

"As long as they're in a bedroom in my house, they are," his mother decided. "When you have your own place, you can have them by the gross and become a gerbil millionaire, but right now, I'm putting you into receivership. Sell off the assets and go into something that doesn't move or smell."

Turning a hobby into something that makes money is a neat coup. Just be sure that in the process, you can manage to continue to enjoy the activity which used to be your hobby. A poor outcome would be creating only a limping little business and, in the process, losing the one pastime which made life worthwhile. In addition, there is the possibility that the people who were pals when it was a hobby they shared with you, will take the dimmest of views when you take the low road and "go commercial."

I Have a Spouse/Friend Who'd Like to Go into Business with Me

Wonderful! Disastrous! Getting entrepreneurial with a spouse or close friend, can be very, very good. And contrariwise, it can be horrid. When it works, it works because the two trust each other, know the fabric of each other's minds, don't have to have meetings about every tiny decision, and have faith that each will work equally hard. One side of a husband-and-wife enterprise maintains that the project would never have been the success it was if the two of them hadn't been involved in it together.

"Apart from anything else, one thing happened virtually every day, and that was when one of us would go home at about 6 p.m.," she recalls. "Could be me going home—could be him. We tried to be fair to each other's exhaustion. So one would go home and the other would say 'tonight doesn't look that bad, I should be home by 7.30. Certainly no later than half eight.' And every single time, the actual arrival was at midnight or later. I wouldn't have believed any husband who kept coming home so late, if I hadn't been in exactly the same position on *my* late nights."

The same husband and wife were amused, one day, to hear their five-year-old son discussing his career plans with a neighbouring parent.

"I'd like a job where I would be home every day for tea," he said.

"Oh, you mean a nine-to-five job," the neighbour said.

"What's nine to five?"

The neighbour explained.

"*Are* there jobs like that?" the youngster asked, wonderingly, his whole concept based on a working pattern more rigorous than your average salt mine.

At least the impression gained by that five-year-old, although it was of an exigent workplace, was also of a positive and happy workplace where the tasks—and the credit for their completion—were shared fairly evenly between his parents.

9

Conversely, there are enterprises started by couples in the first fine careless rapture of mutual trust and love, which have to survive the subsequent break-up of that relationship. Trying to work together when you can no longer stand each other turns each day into a continuum of unproductive misery, but almost equally difficult is any attempt to separate the assets so that justice is done to each of the original contributors while ensuring that the company stays afloat.

I Have a Clear Picture of What I Want to Do, and Nobody's Going to Discourage Me. Even if This Book Says I Shouldn't Go Out on My Own, I'm Still Going to Do It.

Now, we're sucking diesel! Having a clear picture helps. Research suggests that athletes who imagine their way through a moving picture of a race or an athletic meet in their mind before they go out to run it, do much better than equally fit athletes who do not go through this process of "envisaging."

Not allowing anybody to discourage them is a key characteristic of successful entrepreneurs. (It is also, let's be honest, a key characteristic of monumentally UNsuccessful entrepreneurs. Witness John De Lorean, who, having decided he was going to create a business around a car that shrugged its shoulders in order to get its doors open, never really solved the obstacle of the weight of the thing, which was so enormous that petrol consumption was needlessly high, not to mention problems such as the fact that the doors got stuck at public launches of the new vehicle, locking people in for several sweaty hours while the public watched.) The entrepreneur who is going to make it may, indeed *should* listen to everybody who wants to give advice, but ultimately has to follow a personal dream. Thick on the ground, in every sense, are experts and non-experts who, presented with a bright idea, assume that their most important function is to find fault with it. They are equalled in numbers by the experts who know a new idea will not work unless there are six proven precedents for it and who want to cut and paste it into a shape that makes it look more familiar, more orthodox

If you plan to be your own boss, then you may have to do a bit of that cutting and pasting in order to get capital, and it may be a good idea to listen to a few of the nay-sayers, and to read a book like this, in the hope that avoidable mistakes can be prevented and graspable opportunities not missed. Pasteur's observation that "chance favours only the prepared mind," is still true.

But the "prepared mind" is not infallible. There are no guarantees when it comes to being your own boss. You could follow the best advice, have the most pristine paperwork, done at precisely the right time, enter a properly researched market with energy and the right backing—and still come a cropper. If you spend your life trying to avoid making mistakes, you'll never make anything. If, on the other hand, you make it, everybody will say that the signs were always there. They could always tell you were going to be rich and famous.

So have a lash at proving them right. And don't forget to have fun along the way...

2

Starting Small

A small business, as defined by the various state-sponsored bodies dealing with enterprise, is anything employing fifty people or fewer.

This, despite the fact that there are companies employing fewer than twenty people which move millions of pounds around and make a more than a tidy profit. An illogical annoyance of modern business is that if you are a great big unwieldy corporate concrete elephant employing hundreds, turning over millions and making losses, you will often get more respect from financial institutions and you will also have a more assured place within the business establishment than if you're a very small business with a very small turnover and a hefty profit level.

Indeed, when your business is at a purely conceptual stage, you are likely to find yourself being nudged along by the assumptions of others into becoming bigger than you had planned. There is talk about taking a bigger premises, "because if things go as you hope, you'll want to expand in a couple of years' time, won't you?" Once you agree to bigger premises, you find a variation of Parkinson's Law ("work expands to fill the time available for it") in operation. Workers expand and proliferate to fill any space available for them, so that you have an instant overhead before you can start supplying a market with product. It is a bit like doing aerobics with a ten-pound-weight wrapped around each ankle; if you survive and persist, you could become the fittest person on the block, but you could also yank a tendon, dislocate a joint, de-motivate a muscle and put yourself on crutches for six months.

So the first moral, to be articulated to everybody (including you) who wants you to start bigger than you should, is this:

Small Failures Are Less Traumatic and Costly Than Large Failures

Conversely, a small success that wants to grow can always find friends.

The smallest option is the one person business. No, we lie. The smallest option is the one person part-time business.

The world is full of splendid adults who started off in a small way. Not only were they miniaturised at the beginning, hitting the five, six or seven pound mark on the scales, but they didn't commit themselves to proper working hours and contact with the community for quite some time; in the beginning they tended to sleep a lot and cry, which does not require a capital base at all. Moral? If you want to start small, start small. Put your toe in the water. Minimise your risk, and try things out. If necessary, by doing nixers.

Nixers

It's a curious reflection of differing attitudes to enterprise that in Ireland, the word we use for work done outside of and after our normal working day— "nixer"—trails clouds of pejorative implications, whereas the American word for the same practice— "moonlighting"—has connotations of pioneering after-hours glamour.

One of the reasons for the poor image of the nixer, on this side of the Atlantic, is its association with the "black economy." The person who does nixers may not pay tax, may not be insured, may not be honest, may not be properly trained and may be casing your joint in order to pay you a subsequent visit as an unsolicited valuables-removal service. There is also the notion that if you are good enough to work at something, you are good enough to work at it fulltime. Not to mention the fair inference that if you have put in eight hours at the day job, you perform the nixer or night job on the dregs of your energies and talents. The thought that the pilot of your plane may have spent the day working in a nursery and has moved into the cockpit fuelled only by a need for extra cash is enough to send a frisson of fear up the air traveller's spine. But it doesn't happen. Nixers are either full time unrecorded under-the-counter activities, about which we will not speak in this book, or they tend to be routine grinding jobs requiring little in the way of sophisticated skills or judgement, or they are the vehicle in which a staffer hopes to escape, ultimately, from the current fulltime job. When they are the last, a great deal of energy and commitment is on offer by the person offering the part-time service.

That energy and commitment can create a false paradise for the nixer-operator. A nationwide example of this was provided, during the Eighties, by the pirate radio industry, which operated somewhere between the Twilight Zone and the Black Economy, having created a market which it served so well that the removal of stations from the airwaves by legal action resulted in near-riots by young listeners. Pirate radio was popular. In some instances it was also very good, in the sense that it was delivering a stylish popular service to objectively high technical and other specifications. Some of the pirate radio operators, with a view either to the shine on their personal consciences or to longer term operation within the inevitable legal local radio structure that would develop in the Nineties, kept their book-keeping straight, logged the records transmitted, paid their royalties and stayed on the right side of the relevant trade unions. Most of them did not do all of these things, however. In the short term, that meant that they made money—and learned to live in cloud-cuckoo land, where there are only assets, never liabilities, only earnings, never costs. The success stories of illegal pirate radio were not the guaranteed success stories of newly legal local radio, faced, as they were, with the necessity to pay appropriate royalties on music transmitted, forced to pay staff real salaries, required to invest in proper book-keeping, obliged to pay the employer's contributions to health and pension schemes, called upon to contribute a licence fee to the independent authority governing their operations and pushed to put money into premises and equipment in order to meet prescribed standards. Some rolled over and died. Some gulped and re-structured to meet the new context.

What the local radio experience illustrates is the essential falseness of the picture the person doing nixers may develop. If you're earning your living at one job, then it is dead easy for you to cut prices at your second or nixer job in order to compete and win business. Hell hath no fury to match the man who, having used his day job salary to subsidise his undercutting of others in his night-time nixer, then finds the same thing being done to him after he has cut loose from the day job and is dependent, for the care and feeding of his kith, kin and car, on the money made from the former nixer.

Some nixers, or part-time jobs, stay that way forever. A novelist or poet, for instance, has perhaps one chance in fifty thousand of ever earning a full-time living from the pen or typewriter. So the vast majority of writers are something else in real life, and do their writing by getting up earlier in the morning, staying up later at night, grinding away at weekends, or, if they are academics with longer summer breaks, getting thousands of words on paper during the holidays. The day job earns them their living, but, given a free hand, they will describe themselves first and foremost as writers, rather than defining themselves through what they do during their forty-hour working week. This was outrageously true of the novelists and playwrights of the Thirties and Forties who took the train to Hollywood where they were paid astronomical fees to be treated like muck. To a man and a woman, these writers behaved as if film-writing was a grossly inferior nixer job, to be accomplished with both hands metaphorically tied behind one's back and with as much alcohol ingested as is compatible with

17

legible motility of the writing hand. (Dorothy Parker didn't even keep alcohol consumption to this modest level. She would sit, spifflicated, on a couch, while her less talented more sober husband persuaded the next line out of her and typed it on to the page as it slurringly emerged.)

If you want to grow a nixer into a serious alternative to your present job, then:

- Set yourself a deadline. If you don't, you may end up short-changing your present employer but lacking the courage to go out on your own. One of the characteristics common to business winners is that they have a sense of purpose. They know where they're going and they know that it's them who's in charge of getting there. Because business winners are also opportunistic, they may zig and zag a bit as they proceed, but they do not ever sit immobilised in a welter of woolly hopes.

- Use the period between now and your deadline to do research into the reality of turning your nixer into a fulltime job. What would it pay? What would it cost you to deliver the product or service? What's the real market for the product? Once you have established that to your satisfaction, divide it by two or even three. Why? You go to a friend or relative or even a floating voter and ask them a hypothetical question about buying a particular product from you if and when you get around to producing this product, and assuming you can make it at the right price, and you will infallibly get a satisfying number of people to ply you with affirmatives. Of course, they will say. Gosh, they will add. What a good idea. Marvellous. I've always wanted one. Arrive on their doorstep with an actual visible, tangible version of what you talked about and you get a quite different reaction. Research is a wonderful thing, but when people do not have to put their money where their opinions are, they tend to have warm, positive, self-serving opinions that sadly mislead the questioner into an unreal optimum.

- Keep it ethical. There are numerous Managing Directors and General Managers who, once the right button is pushed, will bitterly recount the story of Bobby, who, the year before he set up his own business, ran up a six-figure telephone bill in the company which was employing him, ringing potential customers and suppliers of his planned enterprise at home and overseas. Or they will tell the saga of Jaimie, who ostensibly worked late at night on their behalf, but was in fact running programmes on the computer to help him get the financials for his new enterprise right at the old employer's expense. They may even recount the tale of Mikey who systematically photocopied all the relevant files and did some fifth column-type work in advance of his resignation, so that the week after he set up on his own, several vitally important customers of his previous employer switched and instead became customers of his new firm. Co-incidentally, of course. Innocent shrugging on the part of Mikey. Sustained and venomous bad thoughts of Mikey on the part of his former employers and colleagues.

Freelancing and Sub-Contracting

These two areas tend to overflow into each other, so let's take them as one. A freelance is like a military mercenary. He or she hires on for a particular agreed length of time, and there is no long-term commitment on the freelance's side or on the employer's side. Some freelances work for a number of different employers.

"I had trained with a leading accountancy firm," one freelance accountant says, "and when I qualified, the one thing I was certain about was that I didn't want to become part of this highly structured monolith, even if I earned a lot of money and eventually became a partner. But I also didn't want to be the single accountant in a middling-sized company. I wanted variety. I wanted excitement. Yes, I know accountants are *not* supposed to want that. I know the old joke that an actuary is an accountant who couldn't take the excitement. But while I was training, I had done a few favours, a few bits and pieces of work for small companies that didn't have their own accountant and could never afford one on a full-time basis, and suddenly it hit me. That's what I wanted to do. I wanted to do a few hours here and a few hours there. Be in on the act when companies were at their interesting growth phases. Have total control over my life so I could work thirty six hours at a stretch if I felt like that and then go sailing. In the beginning, I had major problems with my parents, because they felt that failure to be subsumed into one of the big eight accountancy firms was a major setback. They couldn't figure that I could easily have got in, I just didn't want to. It was as illogical to them as being offered a go at assumption into heaven and saying 'Not at this time, thanks all the same.' They were worried sick. Even after three years, when it was perfectly clear that I was making money and was happy as a lark at what I was doing, they were still worried that in some way I was *inappropriately* happy. I wasn't laying down a good foundation for being a pillar of the community, or something. Now that I'm nearly ten years at it, and married, the angle of reproach and fret is different. Now my parents want me to expand and put down corporate roots and 'create something to pass on to your children.' I haven't moved past 'child, singular,' yet—and he's only eighteen months old!"

The aspect of his varied and quite pressured job that this freelance accountant likes best is its division of loyalties. No single boss owns him, rather a series of people in somewhat different businesses regard him as part of their act.

Working for several employers, rather than for one, was part of Linda Cullen's motivation for setting up on her own. Precisely how decidedly she needed to be on her own only became clear as she got through the first difficult year.

"Two years ago I went out on my own and set up a limited company called Video Unlimited," she now recalls. "It was an unnecessary mistake. Not going out on my own, that was the best move I ever made, but setting up a limited company." Linda describes the process as being akin to getting married without living with the person first. The existence of a limited company created only headaches related to paperwork and tax. "It also gave me a false sense of security that encouraged me to incur debt. A limited company must have its own office, its own receptionist, a company car, etc, etc, etc. It would have been wiser and simpler to have started off as a sole trader/freelancer."

Having the backing of a limited company seemed like a solid move. But as Linda Cullen quickly found out, it is just a name—just a status.

"It's a status that can make you feel a failure if you haven't made X amount of money by the end of the year, or God forbid you might make a loss. Which of course I did, not having researched my market properly. I got advice from people in the business of *business* who were dependent on me to forecast my business accurately. Which I didn't do. I didn't allow for error of any sort—business or otherwise. And the forecast I made was for a perfect world with a lot of 'ifs' surrounding it."

It has ultimately turned out for the good. "I'm now discovering the benefits of a limited company— I just did it arse about face."

It took more than a year to recover from the problems resulting from having set up a limited company rather than operating as a sole trader or freelance. Today, Linda Cullen believes it is not necessary to create a business/company to support the career you have chosen.

"True business people are motivated by money,"

she insists. "I am motivated by the type of work I do."

Not all freelances work for a variety of employers. The patterns are changing. A couple of decades back, for example, the National Union of Journalists did not have a separate branch for freelances, because there were too few of them around. When the NUJ eventually got around to setting up a freelance branch, a fair number of the early members were writers or photographers who regarded freelancing as a place or state of punishment or preparation to be endured before being admitted to the staff of a newspaper or broadcasting station, and a fair number of the rest were people who had become disengaged from a staff job and hoped to be sucked back in at some stage. There was relatively little work available for freelances, and so everybody did everything and worked for everybody and kept their pride on a back burner. Today, the Freelance Branch is a busy and populous entity, numbering many members, who despite their freelance status, work exclusively for one employer. They turn up for work virtually every day at some newspaper, where the news desk gives them markings and where they come back to input the story to the computer, rather than returning home to bang it out on their trusty portable.

This kind of long-term freelancing, where someone works more for one employer than for any other, and may even work exclusively for that employer, without, however, joining the employer's fulltime staff, is a close kin to sub-contracting, in that the employer or the main contractor does not, normally, want the client to know very much about the freelance nature of the work done or the sub-contracting of elements of the task. The person awarding the big contract may get very edgy at the thought that a large chunk of the work is not going to be done by the company signing the dotted line of the agreement, but by a quite different company or individual, sub-contracted by the signer. This edginess may be justified, if there is inadequate supervision of the sub-contractor by the main contractor. On the other hand, the work may be better, if the sub-contractor has a special area of expertise, so that what you have is a specialist doing a specialist's task.

Whatever the advantages and disadvantages of the sub-contracting or freelance approach, it is a major trend in many areas of business, because it means that the main contractor doesn't have to carry a huge overhead of staff, and it gives the sub-contractor or freelance at least the illusion of greater freedom and the possibility of better short term money. (None of which is good for the older freelance, who has no premium in a market which favours healthy young people on the make, which does not greatly value experience, and which does not want to know about pregnancy, sick children or the constraints of age.)

What you can make as a freelance depends entirely on the area within which you work. Some freelance activities are effectively ruled, in cost terms, by widely acknowledged fee levels. Unless you have a very specific point of differentiation between what you have to offer, you probably will not make very much more than the norm. If you are in an area so specialised that nobody knows how much you should be paid, but they *do* want your services, it falls to you to decide what you're worth. This is a hellish task, because either you have high self-esteem, in which case you may price yourself out of business, or low self-esteem, in which case you will be in great demand but may have to work treble shifts in order to afford a boiled egg at tea-time.

Striking a rate for your service can be done in all sorts of ways. Try one of these:

1 Decide what you'd like to be paid per year. Now, divide that sum by 1,000. The end result is the figure you should charge for your services per hour. It allows for holidays, weekends and other minor interruptions, and assumes that you will put in a fairly regular number of days' work each and every week.

2 Deciding how much you should be paid per year can be done by multiplying your age by 1,000. Please note that we're not saying you *will* be paid that amount. But you might as well give yourself something to aim at.

3 If you make individual items like sweaters which have a cost attached to them in original materials and in time spent, one rule of thumb for pricing the end result is to multiply the cost of the materials by three. (This assumes you can influence the final price of the item. Knitting items to be included in someone else's range of products and sold under their brand name has traditionally been an option fraught with

exploitation and take-it-or-leave-it minuscule payment.)

Whether you are a freelance, a sub-contractor or a lone consultant, choosing to work as a one-person operation means making a choice between being a limited company or being a sole trader. There are some subtleties stitched into this choice, about which you may need to seek advice. But the essential differences are simple enough. As a sole trader, you have total control, but you also have total responsibility for your own debts, whereas as a limited company, unless you give a personal guarantee to assure a loan when things go wrong, you get to keep the roof over your head and the sheriff doesn't take away your chairs and table.

Whether as a sole trader or as a limited company set up by yourself, what you amount to is a one-person business. This means that you are free from some of the needs which quickly develop if you are in a partnership, a co-op or a company which has more than one employee. You can be a sole trader for life, or use the experience as a phase leading to something quite different. The latter is what Mary Boyle did. Mary had worked for a large state-sponsored body, which, at the end of the Eighties, rationalised, offering voluntary redundancies to staff who wanted out. Mary decided to take the package and try secretarial freelancing, working as a temporary typist in a number of companies for periods as short as one week at a time.

"One of the nicest things about temping is that you don't have to stay anywhere for ever. You're free to take time off in between assignments if you so choose. There's nothing that says you have to work in a place where you don't want to be. It's a good confidence booster—if you feel a bit uncertain in the beginning, after the first few assignments you can walk in to a new post and quite happily take on the world. Experiencing different work practices is invaluable. A consistently high standard of work is expected of the temporary person who has to play the role of the permanent one they're replacing. You've got to do it right or else you find yourself out of work.

"I remember leaving a permanent pensionable position having spent the best part of ten years there and feeling very wary of the outside world—in fact wondering if there *was* an outside world. There was. And it wasn't all bad. For some months I jumped from one temporary assignment to the next with no thoughts of permanent status. Then out of the blue I came to a company that felt very much like home. When they said they'd like to adopt me, I was only too happy to stay.

"The money isn't great—you certainly won't get rich. I suppose the biggest part of the survival kit is adaptability. You'll find yourself dropped in at the deep end of things so it's vital that you have the self assurance to get in there and get on with it. Unfortunately a lot of the time The Temp is looked upon as nothing more than a convenience, delegated to do the things that no one else wants to do, and there's not an awful lot that The Temp can do about it. Some workplaces have a definite territorial feel where some permanent members appear to disregard or even harbour some feelings of resentment towards temporary staff. If you're with a good agency you should be able to air any problems with them and if things get really bad, hopefully you'll get moved to greener pastures. There is no real scope for using one's own initiative even if a job description indicates otherwise so life can get boring at times. Job security is non-existent. There will be times in between assignments when you may find yourself unemployed and signing on in the dole office. I was very happy when I joined a company that treated its temporary staff very much as part of the family and when a position became available for a permanent person, I didn't even have to think about saying yes."

As temps know, to be your own boss you don't necessarily need a premises at all—just a phone. Have skills will travel. And will encounter variety— as Mary Boyle confirms.

Apart from the luxury of working on someone else's premises, as a temp does, the first choice in cheap Square One premises options is your home. It may be possible for you to work from home. Possible— but not necessarily desirable, particularly for women who have been home makers and who are now planning to return to paid employment. The temptation, in that situation, is to say to yourself, "Hey, I'll clear this corner of the sittingroom and set myself up there and it won't cost me anything extra." Lady, lady, think again. Remember Virginia Woolf wanting "A Room of One's Own"? Remember Abigail Adams, wife of the American President, writing plaintively in 1776 that she "always had a fancy for a closet with a window which I could peculiarly call my own." Let us not fudge around on this issue: the wife and mother who tries to set up a new business in the middle of the family home is setting herself a task akin to tackling the Tour de France on a wheelbarrow. That so many women overcome the odds implicit in the gamble is a tribute to those women but should not kid any of the rest of us into thinking it is easy. It is mind-bendingly difficult. Family needs assert themselves in the shape of phone-calls, fights, demands for food, attention or punishment of a third party. When perfect peace breaks out, you notice the dirt on the floor or the odd smell from under the couch. Pals arrive at the door saying that they know they shouldn't interrupt you when you're working away, but they just thought you'd like a break from the hard grind. Window cleaners solicit your permission for them to make your establishment transparent as to its glazing, and *Encyclopedia Brittanica* salespeople emotionally blackmail you to let them provide you with the means permanently and systematically to enlighten your offspring. One female sole trader of our acquaintance was working away when a knock at the front door, absent-mindedly answered, resulted in a gorilla in her hall performing a kiss-a-gram with truly terrifying enthusiasm before she could tell him that the birthday girl was in the house across the road. The fact that the sole trader's husband arrived home from his place of work just as the gorilla had segued his dogged and doggerelled way to the final hairy kiss complicated matters even further.

Planning to prevent gorillas is probably pushing

it a bit, but anyone planning to work from home should make sure that they can:

Create a dedicated work station for themselves which is respected by all other members of the family and which is not in full view of any casual visitor,

and

Create a dedicated time slot for themselves which is similarly respected by all other members of the family and which can be gradually conveyed as meriting respect to other relatives and to friends.

A dedicated work station is easy enough to achieve if, say, you are a good typist planning to produce word-processed theses and other documents. Purchase of an intelligently-designed desk can make the most of a corner space or out of the triangular gap under a staircase, and a good typist's chair with padding and on five wheels will fit neatly into the desk when not in use. (Look for lockable drawers on any desk, and make a practice of covering up documentation in progress when anyone walks into the room; Ireland is a very small place and a client who hears that her work was on display in your sitting-room will not be a happy client.) Think twice about attic conversion. Though the person who converts an attic into an office certainly gains light and charmingly angled ceilings, not to mention a surprisingly large amount of space, they also gain an extra flight of stairs to be negotiated when the representative from An Post arrives wanting a signature on the green slip. Not only is there an additional flight of stairs, but those stairs are often less solid and spacious than the ones that came first time around with the house. If attic conversion is an option, by all means winkle the money out of your bank manager and let builders commence, but arrange the task so that your kids get all of that wonderful space up there, and that you move your new office into what was once their bedroom, on the first floor.

In planning a work space, remember that there are always rules and regulations just waiting in the bureaucratic woodwork waiting to bite you. It may look like a simple proposition; here you are, you have a particular dish you cook like nobody else does, and you have it all worked out that you could probably produce sixty-four of said dish a week and Marks & Spencer would be only strangling themselves with enthusiasm to sell them. In fact, long before you ever get to talk to Marks & Spencer, there may be bye-laws you are infringing by cooking commercially in a family residence. Check it out in advance.

Marks & Spencer, before they even consider your product, will get the screaming meemies at the notion of you producing it in your kitchen. Heart by-pass surgery gets done in places that are sloppier and less sophisticated than the premises M&S demand of their suppliers.

Let's go a step further. Marks & Sparks are lovable little labrador puppydogs compared to the Inland Revenue people, and at some stage, especially if you are a limited company, you're going to have to persuade the Revenue Commissioners that you deserve tax relief on the space devoted to your business, and you'd better have a defensible, provable story to tell, covered in QEDs, because the Revenue Commissioners are about as easy to convince as Boris Yeltsin and they operate from a basic belief that you're trying to cheat the government of its entitlements by pretending that this room or that telephone line is used solely for business when they know for sure that the former is used for illicit poker games and that the latter is used for heavy breathing recreational calls by family members.

After space, the most basic prerequisite to successful working from home is time, and it is the requirement most frequently overlooked. Just as the road to hell is paved with good intentions, the road to disaster in a home-based enterprise is non-specific goodwill on the part of family members. Of course they want you to work and respect your time, but just this once? Making a go of a home office means establishing blocks of time which are sacrosanct and invaded by nothing short of a need to take someone to the casualty ward of a hospital with a minimum of two broken legs. This, by the way, works both ways. Once you have a business up and running, it throws up incidents and problems which are fascinating to the person running the business, but which can become a bore to the other people in the house. "Oh, you're *not* talking shop again?" said testily by a mate or a child is a healthy reminder that your business may be located in your house, but it shouldn't take it over. This caveat applies with extra emphasis to people who take early retirement and set up as consultants in their particular area of expertise, based in their family home. Senior executives who are used to the give-and-take of a big office and even more used to having colleagues or subordinates committed, for one reason or another, to chat or to attentive listening, may, when they start to operate a business out of the family residence, drive the nearest and dearest straight up the wall and down the other side, by constantly invading their space and time and silence.

Having a space of your own does not presume that it must be a space into which you invite others. Your business may require you to have meetings with clients, but those meetings do not have to be on your premises. There are alternatives. You can meet clients on their turf, which may suit them very well, since they do not have to battle traffic to reach you. Hotels will rent small meeting rooms for a reasonable cost for a couple of hours. Check around to find the hotel which is easiest to reach, has car-parking space and is cost-effective. Given a tight enough brief and enough notice, a good hotel will provide a room with a table appropriate to the numbers at the meeting and equip it with flip charts, scratch pads and pencils. It helps, too, if you work out the logistics of ordering coffee or a meal in advance, so that everything is clearly within your control.

Having a Diner's Club Card gives you access to their lounges at major airports, where there is always fresh coffee, comfortable seating appropriate to a small meeting, snacks, a telephone and often a FAX, none of which you pay for as a separate cost—they come with the card. If your business requires you to have infinite capacity for taking planes, then

Diner's Club International Airport Lounges

Country	Airport
Austria	Vienna
Belgium	Brussels
Brazil	Rio de Janeiro
	Sao Paulo Congonhas
	Sao Paulo Cumbica
Colombia	Bogota
England	Heathrow (Terminal 2)
	Gatwick
	Manchester
Germany	Berlin
	Dusseldorf
	Frankfurt
	Hamburg
	Munich
Ireland	Dublin
Israel	Ben Gurion Airport Tel Aviv
Japan	Osaka International
	Narita International Tokyo
Kenya	Jomo Kenyatta International Nairobi
Korea	Seoul Kimpo International
New Zealand	Auckland International
Peru	Lima (Jorge Chavez International)

you will find the Diner's Club lounges in airports all around the world marvellous locations for meetings. (*Small* meetings.)

Meetings are not, of course, the only activities with which even the best-equipped home may find it difficult to cope. Computer services, noisy processes or technical experimentation are unlikely to be achievable in your converted sitting-room corner. But that does not mean you have to commit yourself to major locational overheads. In fact, it means the opposite. If you are a one-person business, devote your creativity to innovative skiving; beg, borrow or steal space that someone else is not fully using.

Keep as your model Edwin Land, the man who invented polarised sunglasses and the instant camera. Long before he had set up the Polaroid company, and several decades before his inventions began to make serious money for him, he needed laboratory space and equipment in which to conduct experiments, accompanied by the scientist who was later to become his wife, named Terre. The two of them, as Land's biographer Peter C Wensberg records, found a no-cost way of reaching the objective. "Before long," Wensberg writes, "Terre was accompanying him on nocturnal visits to a laboratory building at Columbia University. They climbed up a fire escape and went through a convenient window that was usually left unlocked. There for a few hours each night, Land had clandestine access to a well-equipped laboratory." (*Land's Polaroid*)

While we are not positing breaking and entering as a way of getting the space your business needs, we are suggesting that you think laterally about the space problem; along the lines Land himself suggested when he said that great advances tend to be made by people who can "take a fresh, clean look at the old, old problems."

Operating a business on your own can be greatly facilitated by having the right kind of technology. Note that we said "having" rather than "buying." When you're doing a small scale start-up which is unlikely to attract state grants, because you're only planning to employ one person, you should approach any bit of technology with a few crude rules in mind:

- Leasing is better than buying. If you're not sure of your cash flow, and if you can manage it, renting, short term, is better than either leasing or buying. Borrowing is better than either.

- Second-hand is sometimes better than new. It can save you a lot of money, if the machine has been re-conditioned by a reputable company and carries a guarantee. If you keep your eye out for the auctioning of equipment from companies that have gone under, you may turn up machinery which did not die of old age (which is why many companies put a machine on the second-hand market) but was rendered unemployed through no fault of its own.

- Quiet is better than noisy. A cheap noisy machine will not only make you as popular as Typhoid Mary within the house, and annoy the hell out of your neighbours if used at unusual hours (which is precisely when you, as a lone operator, may want to use it) but it will need to be turned off or unused when phone calls are being made. If you are forced to buy a noisy typewriter, bed it down on several layers of foam padding to absorb the keystroke clack.

- Nearby is often better than on location. Many suburban newsagents now have photocopy machines available for customers' use, and FAXes are increasingly accessible through instant print shops and other similar operations. Always choose an instant small expense rather a continuous grinding overhead.

However, a FAX in your home means people can get to you even when you are not at base, and that you can have a response waiting for them when they arrive for work the following day. Even more than the computer, the FAX has made professional home-working an appealing option and contributed to the fulfilment of the prophecies of Alvin Toffler and John Naisbitt that we'll all move out of our clogged, polluted cities and operate high-powered businesses in rural isolation. Naisbitt, for one, exemplifies what he predicts as a trend; having had a bestseller (*Megatrends*) in 1982 with researcher and later wife Patricia Aburdene, he moved on to operate an international consultancy on coping with change and the future, while preparing the follow-up book, *Megatrends 2000*, which became a bestseller in 1990. The couple have a research office with two employees in Washington DC, which, if they really have to, they'll visit perhaps once a year, staying in touch, for the most part, by phone, FAX and modem from their mountain home/workstation in rustic mountainy Colorado.

There is a clever little switch available which allows a phone and a FAX to operate, at different times, from the same telephone line, thus saving the subscriber the cost of a second line. Bitter experience informs us when we suggest that you avoid this clever little switch and spend the money on a second phone line. Bitter experience says that you can get very tired of having to listen very carefully to the noises emitted by your phone and your FAX in order to find out which of them wants to communicate at any given time. Your FAX sounds more like an old fashioned phone than an old fashioned phone does, and is easily discouraged. So someone tries to send you a FAX, you get confused and answer the phone, the phone screams at you in electronic contempt, you put down the phone and go to wherever you have the switch and move it to one side, and if you're very lucky, the person eager to do some transmitting will try again, in which case you will fall on their message with glad cries and forget to switch the FAX back to PHONE, so that when the baby-minder rings up in a rage because you are later than you promised you would arrive at the baby-minder's house to collect your toddler, the baby-minder, who is vexed to start with, is rendered incoherent by the response of the phone in your house, which still thinks it is a FAX because nobody has told it any different, and which, accordingly, shrills at the caller like an express train about to murder someone at an unmanned level crossing. Get lots of information before you invest in a FAX.

A machine for taking messages is also needed by the one-person business. Let us revise that, marginally. The optimum answer, if the desired respondent is out of the house, is from a human being. If you have a human being handy who is prepared to do a civil job on the phone for you when you have to be out, this is much better than any answering machine. We know of one Information Manager for a news-making controversial organisation who is in constant demand by reporters, and who has never installed an answering machine, because his daughter, now in her early teens, has for years happily taken on the responsibility of greeting callers civilly and taking legible messages. The callers end up charmed and placated, even if they have an urgent information requirement, in a way they would not be charmed and placated by a machine.

If, however, you do not have a charming relative or friend who is always willing and ever present, then the next best option is a telephone answering machine. Leave a simple, uncomplicated message in the tone of voice in which you normally talk, and have a routine check of the machine the moment you come in the door. Calls should always be returned as quickly as possible, just as letters should be answered without delay. If not out of courtesy, then as part of marketing. It annoys and even insults a potential client to be ignored or have a query postponed, and what is even more damaging to you is that it creates an impression that you are neither professional nor eager for their business.

Some telephone answering technology allows you to get in touch with your messages without going home to collect them, a service which, if you are forced to do a lot of travelling, can be valuable.

Telephone-answering technology should never be used simply as a bucket into which fall messages that arrive when you are out. It should also be used as a time-management tool, so that the machine gets switched on, not only when you are physically out of the building and unable to respond to an incoming call, but also when you are physically present in the building but engaged in an important task. Let's say that you are preparing a proposal which, if it hits the right note, will solve many of your cash-flow problems in the coming year. That task is just as demanding of your full and undivided attention as is the normal meeting which would take you away from your office. So? So turn on the telephone-answering machine and don't allow incoming calls to break your train of thought. Your machine should be one of those which lets you hear, and if necessary talk to, a caller. Making the best use of this capacity requires discipline. There is no point in being able, in effect, to eavesdrop, unbeknownst, on all calls coming to your phone, if you do not, having eavesdropped, rigorously select the few to be talked to out of the majority who will be responded to at some later stage.

A car phone can be very useful and a time-saving boon, as long as you buy one of the units which has a remote microphone and so can be operated in totally hands-off mode. Cellular phones can be expensive. For the man or woman operating a consultancy without staff support, however, they are invaluable, in their facilitation of instant problem-solving contact with clients and in their capacity to convey to clients your constant availability to them.

On conventional phones, Telecom Eireann has a "call following" service which costs peanuts and which is extremely helpful to the one person operation. By using PHONEPLUS you can arrange to have calls rerouted so as to catch up with you somewhere you know you are going to be during that day; your client's office, perhaps. Another handy device is the "call waiting" system, whereby someone ringing your one telephone line does not go away, cross, because you were engaged. Two beeps lets you know there's another call on the line. This call can be answered in total privacy by the push of a button while holding the first call.

Whether or not you need a computer depends on the nature of your business, but the fact is that there are few businesses these days—especially businesses which are not heavily staffed—which do NOT need a computer. Even a simple computer, given the right software and a good print unit, can produce impressive letters and can do them in "mail/merge" which makes promotional mail-shots a joy to orchestrate. A little extra software, allied to appropriate training, lets the one person operator do their own book-keeping and preliminary accountancy work, permits the drafting of "desktop publishing" documents and provides an electronic diary and flagging system which reminds the operator to pay particular bills or contact specific people for follow-up meetings. It also lessens the amount of storage space needed, since keeping several hundred documents in "hard copy" form, i.e., on paper, takes a lot more square footage than does storing the same amount of data on a hard or soft disc.

The trick, in analysing whether or not you need a computer, and if you DO need a computer, which is the best to buy, is to avoid advisers with a vested interest who will cost money. This sounds simple, but is quite difficult. Go to a company which makes computers and they will inevitably find that you not only need a computer, but you very clearly need their particular Model Xcz22++. Go to a company which sells everybody's computers, and they will find that you need a computer, and will come up with a recommendation which just happens to be available from their store.

This is where our experience is not bitter—for once—but is devious. We start with a national statistic. Ireland has arguably the biggest proportion of high-tech graduates and high-tech students in any country in Europe and possibly in the world. Every second twenty-year-old in this country is coming apart with knowledge about computers. Ergo, everybody's younger brother or sister is a computer freak. Or is best friends with a computer freak. Just send out a vague message saying that you want to talk to a computer freak and it may be worth a few quid and you will find them on your doorstep like milk bottles. Sit down with them and tell them all about the kind of business you plan to run, the frail brevity of the shoestring on which you plan to run it, and the problems you think might be solved by a computer, and let them bounce the information around. If they know their stuff and if they ask you the right questions, they may come up with the answers to your problems. (By the way, if you don't feel you have problems, prepare to be irritated by the endless nattering on that computer freaks do about "solutions." For some odd reason, they never talk about computers or machines or technology any more. They talk about solutions. Nobody else talks like this. You don't hear accountants talking about doing your audit "on their solution.")

Most of the needs of a start-up one-person business are simpler and cheaper than a computer. Office furniture is always going cheap, somewhere, because some other unfortunate entrepreneur has just folded his tent and slunk away. Look up the Yellow Pages and you will find furniture sellers who specialise in second-hand office chairs, tables, desks and filing cabinets. Unless you are unable to function in an aesthetic disaster area, you can equip your workplace dirt cheaply with unmatched and somewhat bruised hand-me-downs.

You will also need paper. Depending on your business, you can buy generic invoice forms and simply type your company or personal name in at the top, or you can have a logo (a symbol or design which visually differentiates your company from all others) designed and printed onto your own paper. The latter, if done well, can create an instantly identifiable and pleasing image for your operation, and can be personally reassuring as well. (Don't knock it. There are mornings, when you're your own boss, when looking in the mirror is not enough to convince you that you exist and are a worthwhile entity, and when an elegant compliment slip with your name on can constitute a clean adult comfort blanket.)

Having corporate designs created and printed onto paper is one of those ostensibly simple tasks that swells invisibly and costs money you never knew you had, for the very good reason that you *didn't* have it. Some of our best friends are designers and printers, but we have learned that when it comes to money, they can go through an awful lot of it. So if you decide to have a logo created, fish around before you pick a designer. If you like an existing logo, ring up the company and ask them who did it for them. They may tell you that their advertising agency created it, or they may reveal that a freelance designer developed it, or they may tell you to get stuffed. The lone designer is the most positive answer, because you can sit down with a lone designer and confess your poverty in detail and agree with him the outer limits of what he will charge you. Get him to do a rough, rather than a final piece of artwork, so that you are not locked into a huge cost for a design with which you may not be satisfied. If you persuade a designer to do work for you for half nothing, and the end product is both a delight and a substantive help in establishing and positioning your business, go back and use that designer again and pay him or her better the next time around. One-person operations are very vulnerable, and their creativity is not always properly rewarded.

In briefing your designer, by the way, keep two things in mind. If you decide simply to use your own name for the company, it may facilitate introduction to potential customers if there is some kind of tag line on the notepaper, describing what you do:

TERRY STEPHENSON LTD
Frog Catchers and Exporters

The second thing to keep in mind is that initials and meaningless names are a pain in the ass. Initials are loved by the kind of people who play crosswords filled with acronyms, and those people are rarely entrepreneurial pioneers. (We have no evidence whatever to support this prejudice, but we're going to hold on to it, anyway.) *You* know that your company is called ENDS because it stands for Environmentally Nascent Development Services Ltd., but why should a customer put himself through a tedious set of barriers in order to come to terms with what you do if you should really be calling yourself Recyclers Anonymous? A few companies, having been around a long time, decided that using initials would pin down their image less precisely and in a less limiting way than the old full name. So International Business Machines became IBM and National Cash Registers became NCR. So far, so good. Then a whole lot of dubious conglomerates which didn't particularly want anybody to know for sure who they were and how vast and diverse was the scope of their interests also went into the initials business. The confusion level was rising, just a bit. Finally, a welter of innocent little companies that wanted to look impressive and well-established grabbed a handful of letters and allowed as how they would be happy to have themselves summed up by that handful. Of course, if you want to, you can name your company using three or four initial letters. Most people in business will nod, wisely. The authors of this book wish you wouldn't. Because you should love your own business almost as much as you'd love a kid—and want it to be loved by others, ditto. And not many of us initialise our offspring.

About meaningless names, we will give you just two examples to inform and confuse you. A man took over an American company named United Airlines. Renamed it Allegis. Before customers had got over the "WHA'?" stage, the man at the top was gone from the top and the company was back to being United Airlines.

The moral of this example is clearly that thinking up meaningless names for an enterprise is a damnfool activity.

So we move to the second example. Here, the location was Japan, and the entrepreneur was in a green field situation.

He had a new company that nobody had ever heard of. He had a perfectly good family name. But he decided to make up a name which meant nothing. He picked Sony. It worked.

Multinationals spend millions of pounds, dollars or yen to arrive at great names for products or companies under their umbrella. A Swiss confectionery company recently commissioned a trademark specialist to come up with a new name for a Swiss chocolate bar. The company's computers spewed out random names, and the company's creative specialists dreamed up a slew of others. Out of the total of 350 suggestions, more than three hundred were turned down by the client because they didn't give him the warm and fuzzies, and all but two of the remainder turned out already to exist and be registered somewhere else in the world. Which reminds us; once you have picked your company name, check that someone else did not beat you to it, because if they did, you have no rights to it and they could sue you for infringing copyright. (And win: Rolls Royce, to quote but one household name, gets very litigious with companies which describe themselves as "the Rolls Royce" of a particular trade.) The Companies Registration Office & Registry of Business Names, which is based in Dame Street, Dublin, Telephone (01) 614222 will tell you if a name already exists in this country and the equivalent office overseas will tell you if a name is copyrighted in any nation into which you are thinking of selling your wares.

Once you have decided on a name and on the design to go with it, and have the "camera ready" artwork in your hand, the next step is to pick a printer. Do not start with the bigger plants, because they won't want to know you. Go to at least three smallish printers and ask for estimates. Pick the one who seems most interested, as long as that one isn't also the most expensive, and get the agreed price in writing before they start.

Precisely what bits of paper you actually need is related to the nature of your business. One general hint, however, is to get compliment slips which are about a third of A4 size paper. They fit into an envelope and can double as notepaper when you don't want to type out a full letter to someone, but still want to leave a good impression.

So now you have all the raw materials in place, you have decided that your strength is in handling work, not workers, and you are ready to be your own boss—and nobody else's boss. Much of the rest of this book will be of relevance to you, so read on. But before you do, two considerations which are more important to you than to companies with more employees.

The first is managing your dependencies. Which is a slightly posher way of saying "Don't put all your eggs in one basket," because the basket can fall apart. A friend of ours who had been in advertising in the capital moved to a small provincial town a few years ago, and quickly worked out that she wasn't going to be able to do much copy-writing for money in this town. But a great new electronics factory was being built at the time she arrived, and recruitment was beginning to get under way to ensure that when the plant opened, the staff would be ready, trained and eager. So many of the local people wanted CVs done, in order to impress the Personnel Manager of the factory. Our friend decided that this was a version of copy-writing, quickly refined her inter–viewing skills so she could help job candidates establish to an interviewer's satisfaction what were their main personal selling points, and turned her word processor and laser printer to this new market. For almost two years she did very well indeed. Then she hit a wall, and her income dropped so suddenly and so totally that paying the electricity bill became a problem. No, she had not suddenly started to do poor work. But the factory had very nearly filled all its vacancies. That, on its own, would not have caused her major difficulties, but it was complicated by the fact that several observant people in the town had decided that a knack for ordering facts, allied to intelligent copy layout using a word processor, added up to pretty good CV production, and they had set up in opposition to her. None of them was doing as well as she had in the beginning, but now, a diminishing market was being split into five or six pieces. Our friend had to move quickly to establish other services which could be sold in this locale.

A variation on this theme is where you become dependent on a single client. Occasionally, there is no choice in this, and a consultant works happily for one company and is kept busy by that company's needs for several years. Ideally, however, single-company dependency should be avoided, and single-person dependency is positively lethal. That's where you work not only for one company, but for one person within that company. It happens. It also happens that the one person for whom you work is not that keen to let other people in the company know how it is that you improve his performance, so he says very little about what you actually do, and the rest of the staff, consequently, are deeply suspicious of you and paranoid about what you're really at.

If your individual client gets hit by a tractor or eaten by a virus or his ticker stops short, never to go again, then the rest of the company will pull together as one man (or woman) in order to do you down the moment the official mourning is over. Spread relationships. Don't threaten your immediate client's subordinates. Don't give lip to your immediate client's colleagues. Establish networks, for you never know the day nor the hour.

Of course, it could, the Lord between us and all harm, be *your* little ticker that decides to make like My Grandfather's Clock, which brings us to the last vital element you need to build into your planning as a one-person business; what the aircrew call "your comfort and safety." The one person business needs circuit breakers. The boss needs something other than tranquillisers or booze; totally remove them from the pressures of the daily routine. It is important that those circuit breakers be built in from the very beginning, rather than postponed until things get off the ground, things get better, or profits start to be made.

Oddly enough, sleep is not the first of those circuit breakers. The myth that everybody needs eight hours sleep is precisely that—a myth. Some people certainly need eight hours sleep, but a great many people need less. And if the people who are used to eight hours are rationed down to seven and a half for six months, not only do they not die or become less productive or get depressed, the reverse of all those things happens. They stay alive, they are much less likely to become depressed, and they have more time in which to accomplish their day's work. So if you suffer a bit from insomnia at crucial stages in your company's development, welcome to the club and use the extra time you have been handed intelligently.

You're less likely, even when justifiably anxious, to suffer insomnia if you get regular exercise. Walking, running or swimming several days a week will also keep your heart and lungs in good working order and help you control your weight. (That last sentence was put in there because the medical profession told us to. Only one of the writers believes in it. The other thinks being a chocolate-eating slob is a lot more fun than sweating your way around running tracks.)

A pastime which is radically different from your job can also be a help. And do not forget holidays. Fortnights in the sun, covered in Factor 25. Single weeks in France, learning how to produce gourmet meals. Three-week stretches in the mist outside Spiddal. When you are starting a one-person business, holidays seem an almost frivolous consideration. Eighteen months down the road, when you have still not worked out how to get away for a short spell, it begins to look not so much a frivolity, more a desperate need. Taking a holiday, even when you have clients who are wonderfully dependent on you, is relatively easy. You decide when you're taking it—several months in advance— and you tell them, several months in advance. You tell them that you have told them, remind them. And go.

3

Meet My Entrepreneurial Personality

An awful lot of bull gets talked about "entre–preneurial personalities" and an "enterprise culture." The person who wants to be their own boss can be pressured by all this stuff. They get to believe that they must carry along a series of identifiable entrepreneurial characteristics, like designer luggage. "Hi, I'm Mary Smyth and this is my entrepreneurial personality."

There is a marvellously uniform consensus about what makes an entrepreneur.

- It's the guy who is driven by a single idea and has already registered it as copyrighted in the Patents Office by the time he's thirteen.

- It's the girl who created a little company when she was in second class to sell comics during the summer holidays.

- It's the man who did engineering *and* accountancy, so as to know how the machinery works and how the books work, too.

- It's the scion of a family which majored on achievement, where kids were pushed to discover themselves.

- It's the charismatic leader who displaces air the moment he walks into a room.

- It's the visionary risk-taker who does not acknowledge the possibility of failure.

The entrepreneur may be one of those people, but there's no law saying that's the way it has to be. Study statistics on entrepreneurship long enough, and you will be able to extrapolate a figure which may get you a headline on a dull news day ("Study reveals majority of entrepreneurs 5'7" or over") but which is of no use whatever to someone thinking of becoming their own boss. Indeed, it may be de-motivational. We're all suckers for quizzes where we fill in the questions, tot up the coded answer values, and discover that we are only average in the sex-pot department or that we are outstanding as spellers. The only danger is when you find that the result of the quiz apparently disqualifies you from doing what you had hoped to do.

Please don't read this chapter to find out what disqualifies you from being your own boss. *Nothing* disqualifies you from being your own boss. If you want to do it badly enough, and attack the project in a persistently organised way, you'll succeed.

What this chapter may do for you is point up some interesting patterns showing whence entrepreneurs, up to now, have been most likely to come.

Go back fifty or a hundred years, and what you find is that invention was often the mother of entrepreneurship. Someone developed a car or a plane and set up a plant to manufacture what they had invented. As time went on, one of three things happened:

- The inventor was always more interested in inventing than in manufacturing and making money, and so other people turned the inventions into big business.

- The inventor (Henry Ford, although he was only one of dozens of contemporaries who copped on to the potential of the motor car) applied his brain to the process of manufacturing (conveyor-belt assembly, in Ford's case) and marketing ('you can have any colour you want, as long as it's black') and became a millionaire.

- The world decided that it could happily live without a particular invention, and the project went broke.

The last of the three happened much more often than the first two, and when it happened, it was sometimes attributable to nothing more than unfortunate timing. For instance, the prospects for success were good when an inventor with a good track record set out to devise an attractively priced, portable and technically ingenious instant moving picture camera and playback unit. The company which embarked on manufacturing the final design was known for quality. The product went out into the market place in its shiny new case and died a spectacular death. Why? Because at that very time, the marketplace had been invaded by portable video cameras and domestic playback units which were affordable and even more "instant" than "instant" film could ever be.

In the last twenty years, the inventor-turned-entrepreneur story has not always been a happy one. Witness Steve Jobs, the man who, in his garage, invented the first of the Apple computers and gave birth to a new way of thinking about information technology. The inventor became an entrepreneur, and was successful up to a point. The point came at the middle of the eighties, when Pepsi's Marketing whizz, John Scully, was brought in to direct Apple into the Nineties. Scully fairly quickly and fairly publicly indicated that the qualities which had made Jobs so successful as an inventor and boss of a small growing, guerrilla-like enterprise were precisely the qualities which were endangering the future of the substantial market presence into which Apple had developed. Having started as bosom buddies, they were daggers drawn within months, and Jobs was gone from the top not long afterward.

Sir Clive Sinclair, the high-tech British genius who was instrumental in pushing the computer world into cheapness and portability, was not able permanently to mate the functions of inventor and boss, coming a cropper over an electric car which couldn't be brought to the market at the right time, at the right price and in the right numbers.

In the past couple of decades, not only have entrepreneurs *not* tended to be high-profile inventors, but they have tended to develop smaller businesses which were variations on an existing theme, rather than radical visionary ventures. So we have seen nameless individuals who have looked at the delivery of information within cities and said to themselves "Posting a letter to a place six miles away and having it arrive a few days later is not as useful to business people as giving it to a guy on a motorcycle and having it delivered within minutes at a somewhat higher cost" and who developed courier businesses as a result of that thought process. Within a couple of years, those courier services became so much a part of the texture of big city life that it's now difficult to remember what life was like beforehand, when there were no hard-working Hells Angels dripping rainwater on the receptionist's carpet and shouting incomprehensibilities into the two-way radios on their chests.

Courier service companies are variations on an existing theme, rather than creative inventions of a speculative brain; and that's the reality of most of today's new businesses. They are not set up by inventors of a better mousetrap. They are new or oblique approaches to existing businesses, which in turn means that the old pressure on entrepreneurs has lessened. You can be your own boss these days without being a risk-taking, swashbuckling dreamer. In fact, as you'll find later in this book when we get to problems/opportunities like bank managers, the less you dream, swash and buckle, the better your chances of venture capital.

There is more entrepreneurship about, these days, and a wider variety of traits and characteristics which can be interpreted as typical of people who end up as their own boss. Or, to put it another way, there is no psychological test, no investigative process of fitting shapes into other shapes, which will give a worthwhile advance indication of whether or not someone has what it takes to set up and run their own business.

"There is a great deal which is equivocal and inconclusive about the trait approach to entrepreneurship" was how one leading industrial psychologist put it in a 1986 review of *The Entrepreneurial Personality*. The same psychologist had earlier pointed out that the traits people have or claim to have don't seem to correlate closely with how they behave in real life when opting to work for someone else or start a business on their own. The British Small Business Research Trust, in a 1990 monograph, *The Making of Entrepreneurs*, waved a dismissive hand at all of the "traits" and "characteristics" scene, pointing to quite different factors as significant in entrepreneurship:

"The frequency with which the self-employment option is chosen appears to depend greatly upon two key factors," say SBRT. "First, the range or absence of alternative economic roles available to the individual. Thus, downturns in the labour market appear to result in upturns in the numbers of people becoming self-employed and vice versa. Second is the availability of role-models, particularly within the aspiring entrepreneur's own family."

The first of these factors would seem to be partly a function of culture and of scale; the Depression years of the 1930s did not breed huge numbers of individual entrepreneurs. America's displaced dustbowl-farming family's limits of initiative were frequently expressed by their putting themselves and their remaining belongings into a car and heading in the general direction of a town large enough to have soup kitchens and perhaps the opportunity to sell apples to sympathetic passersby. Recessions in more recent times have generated a different and less disabling form of shakeout. A large company hitting lean years may shed workers but emigration from the family home is not an inevitable concomitant and the new unemployed person is less likely to be old and single-skilled since the worker most likely to be shed is the most recently employed, on the Last In, First Out principle. That worker may be young, educated and reluctant to see the firing as anything but an impersonal acting-out of an employment dynamic, and may, as a result, be not only undefeated, but motivated and even bankrolled to start up a brand new enterprise. Oddly enough, in later years, this particular entrepreneur may not, in telling his or her own success story, include the firing from an earlier job as an important element. Studies of people who started their own business having been fired from someone else's, show that founders of business usually report what is the most socially acceptable reason for their start-up. So they talk about their ambition, their desire for self-expression, or their hunger to own their own Maserati. They do not always talk about getting the boot from the previous employer, even though at least one survey turned up figures underlining that 30% of a group of people who had started up their own business had quit their earlier jobs *without* a clear game plan for their future and 13% had been shown the door by their previous employer because of a plant closure or for some other reason.

In this regard, their sensitivity is often matched by the company which did the firing. American language analyst William Lutz has noted a growing unwillingness among big companies to call a spade a spade and a firing a firing when crafting a press release for media and public consumption. Lutz has found companies which describe this operation in terms varying from "downsizing our personnel" to "selectively improving our operational capacity." He quotes Sun Oil as rejecting the word "layoff." "We don't characterise it as a layoff," they said. "We're managing our staff resources. Sometimes you manage them up, and sometimes you manage them down." On which Lutz commented: "Congratulations, you've just been managed down, you staff resource, you!" (William Lutz, *Doublespeak*)

The survey which found that entrepreneurs were not always eager to acknowledge being fired as an initial factor in their later success, also drove a horse and cart through the popular idea that entrepreneurs leave their earlier jobs because they are driven people with an immutable ideal of being their own employer. In-depth interviewing revealed that, in fact, 40% would have left their previous jobs even if they had never become entrepreneurs—they just didn't like that particular job.

It does seem that companies and industries that are afflicted with periodic crises spawn entrepreneurs more readily than do stable and well-managed businesses. This is also true of industries and state-sponsored bodies at the plateau stage of their corporate history. They have done the bulk of the growing that they're going to do, and are now top-heavy with highly qualified middle and upper managers who are slightly too old to want to compete in the open market, but who are slightly too young to retire. Attractive early retirement or voluntary redundancy packages within such organisations can serve as a last chance at entrepreneurship for employees who might never otherwise break out of what have been described as "fur-lined mousetraps" to take the risks of going it alone.

Certainly, the thought of going it alone is markedly less seductive to employees in large corporate entities which are still on the grow and which therefore continue to offer promotion opportunities to the ambitious. Smaller companies which are well-managed and stable also fulfil some of the personal needs typical of entrepreneurs, because they may afford at least some of their employees a sense of shaping and influencing the direction and product of the company, so the "I'm only a cog in a wheel and nobody ever tells me anything" syndrome does not happen. Nonetheless, the man or woman who sends in the letter of resignation and decides to be their own boss is much more likely to have come from a small firm than from a very big firm, apparently because, within a small firm, it is possible to get a better grasp of how the whole thing works than it is for an employee segregated into one specialist department in a much larger firm. It may also be easier to develop a sense of possibility. After all, when you've been employed as a barman for a few years, you have had the chance to come to terms with Purchasing, Pricing, Marketing, Customer Services and Staff Relations. You may even have come to terms with the exigencies of Security, if yours is one of the phone numbers the alarm company rings when the burglar alarm goes off. So if you want to set up a pub, it is a challenge which you feel you could handle. If, on the other hand, you have been working in the ale kegging plant of a brewery, you may be very skilful, but in a much narrower field, have had relatively little opportunity to learn the other operations within the plant, and as a result the prospect of setting up a brewing operation may rightly seem a challenge you're just not up to.

The job you work at before you set up your own business seems to be a lesser factor in the success of that business than does your family background. (Let us emphasise again, here, that we're not saying you will not make it unless you come from a particular family background. We are saying that a pre-ponderance of entrepreneurs, in the last few years, has tended to come from a particular configuration. No more than that.)

This configuration is not confined to any one country in the industrialised west:

• In 1987, Cooper and Dunkelberg did a survey of owner/managers in the USA. Almost two thous-and individuals were surveyed. Just under half of them had started their own business. 50 % of those entrepreneurs had come from homes where a parent or a guardian owned a business.

- In Belgium, in the same year, Donckels and Dupont examined 400 new small businesses. They found that 45% of those businesses had been started by people who had an entrepreneurial father, 19% by people whose mother had been an entrepreneur.

- In Ireland, the year before, P. O'Farrell, studying data from manufacturing entrepreneurs on behalf of the Irish Management Institute, noted that 46% of them had a self- employed father.

Analysts of studies like the ones quoted suggest that it isn't just that people coming from families wherein there is a tradition of entrepreneurship are more likely to start their own business; they are also somewhat more likely to succeed in the experiment if they have a network of family and friends who are themselves self-employed.

"It's only retrospectively that you notice things like that," one man running a ten-person business for the last five years told us. "I only realised it when I went to a school reunion and got sitting next to a former classmate of mine who is now a surgeon. He was saying that the final years of his training—I think he meant the intern years, when you're on duty for, like, days at a time and you're going around sleepwalking but knowing people's lives are depending on you—he said those years were so bad that he could never have survived them if both his mother and his father hadn't been doctors themselves and hadn't gone through the same thing. And I'm sitting here listening to him and I suddenly realise that my experience has been the mirror-image of his, except that mine was in running my own business, and my 'key relative,' if you could call it that, was my father on his own. It's not that I ever took my problems to him, or that the business he ran was in any way like the business I started up. It was more that I had a sense of priorities. I kind of knew what to be scared of. Because when you're a novice in business, every bit of paper from the Revenue Commissioners looks like a death sentence, every envelope with the Bank's logo on the flap looks like an ultimatum, unless you've got a kind of subconscious memory of hearing your father talk about things like that. For example, I remember when I was very small, overhearing my father say to my mother that he was ready to split one of his staff who had answered a phone-call from the bank manager when my Dad wasn't there and had caused him big heartburn by telling the bank manager some extra detail that my father didn't believe the bank manager needed to know. When I was setting up on my own, that memory, more than any of the books I read, or courses I attended, served me well, because I made a small rule that nobody but me was ever to talk to the bank manager. As a result, he and I have developed a relationship that has absolutely no misunderstandings in it. I'm sure there's oodles of other ways that I do things, without knowing I do them, because my father's way of operating seems most logical to me. I'm also sure that there's oodles of ways that I do things the exact opposite to the way he would do them, because I didn't like the way it worked in his place."

Whether the young entrepreneur credits the example of an entrepreneurial parent as a major contributory factor in their own success, or feels that it is all no more than a coincidence, the fact is that, internationally, the founders of small businesses are more likely to have a self-employed or owner/manager parent than are the rest of us. According to Britain's Small Business Research Trust, the self-employed and the founders of small businesses also seem more likely than the rest of the population to have other relations and friends operating within small businesses or to have previously worked in small businesses themselves.

"Our findings...show that small firms breed other small firms both through inter-generational links and through the 'incubation' of other new firms via their former employees," say SBRT. "Finally, al–though we are not able to predict which among the large numbers of entrepreneurs that start a business each year will join the relatively few able to grow their small firm into a large one, we are beginning to understand more about the origins and motivations for enterprise. Other research... indicates that the prime motivation of the small business owner is not money but self-expression and achievement. The choice of the small business route to the realisation of these aims, it seems, will be determined by sociological rather than psychological factors. Socialisation patterns, particularly during childhood, but also later in life, appear to go a long way towards explaining the origins of enterprise."

Nobody seems to have a handle on where precisely education fits into all of this. By education we mean passage through the educational system up to and including third level. Training—particularly training aimed at creating entrepreneurs—is quite another matter and will be dealt with in Chapter 4. One observer of Ireland's growing enterprise culture told us very decidedly that people who went through general Arts degrees were never any good as entrepreneurs, whereas you could find accountants in key positions in large and small enterprises all around the country. Certainly, we found that accountants are frequently at the helm in growing enterprises. We did not observe that accountants, more than any other single profession, tended to *start* companies. The route is often more circuitous than that. The accountant may be called in by the person who has an idea for a new business, on the basis that the entrepreneur knows nothing about the funding and structuring of a company, and may from quite early on become involved as a shareholder, director or executive. Alternatively, because so many accountants work as consultants to growing or troubled businesses, they may get sucked out of their parent company and into the one which they have served as consultants. (This pattern is not, of course, confined to accountants. Many multi-national corporations setting up in Ireland over the last quarter century ended up wooing into their man—agerial hot seat the executive who had been taking care of them on behalf of one of the national development agencies.)

But in some cases, the people who set up the business have neither accountancy nor any other degree and no direct experience of the type of business they set up—yet they make a success of it. Take Aibhlín McCrann, who decided to set up a florist's shop.

"Friends gaped incredulously when they heard the news," she laughs. "Married to a farmer, teaching Irish in a Community School and playing the harp certainly didn't equip me to start up a business. They thought I was mad. Maybe I was. Their reactions made me all the more determined to push on with the idea—a plan concocted with my husband and a couple of friends as we sat around the fire sipping wine. No, not an alcohol-induced fantasy. Simply an idea inspired by an urge to make a few bucks for I also had this notion that I'd never get rich working for other people. So the decision was made. A shop for rent in the area. What to put in it? Not a travel agency. Too dicey. Not a restaurant. Too many of them. Not a beautician. Too specialised. And not a pageful of other things until we eventually hit on a flower shop."

The area seemed right for Aibhlín's enterprise. The customers were there. There were several hospitals, churches and undertakers close by and there wasn't another florist within five or six miles.

"We blissfully disregarded the fact that we hardly recognised a rose from a carnation. Neither had any of us set foot in a flower shop more than once or twice. Never mind the finer points like buying the flowers, arranging them, making bouquets or assembling wreaths. The staff could tell us. And that's exactly what happened. We interviewed lots of expert and experienced people, asked lots of pertinent questions and at the end of it all knew a lot more about what we needed to know."

Ten years, two flower shops and one baby later, the flower business is no more than a line on Aibhlín's CV.

"It was sold as a going concern but I still feel the intense cold at six in the morning as I picked my way through boxes of flowers at the Dublin Flower Market. The sense of camaraderie as we sat in Paddy's Bar munching the rasher sandwiches and drinking piping hot tea after the buying was done. The clackety clack of the till on a hectic Xmas Eve. The frantic rush to deliver Valentine's Day orders. The look of utter bemusement on a customer's face as she received a bouquet together with a kiss from our delivery man—an Austrian boyfriend of my sister, whom we had convinced that this was the way it was done in Ireland. The look of utter horror on his face when he discovered it was a con. The sheer euphoria of selling something to people who wanted to buy; a far cry from teaching Irish to unwilling kids. Delivering a bouquet to a large house in a well-to-do area and being told by the housekeeper to go to the tradesman's entrance. Me!!!

Did I make my fortune? Not really. Was it worth it? You betcha!!!!"

One of the factors helping Aibhlín and her husband was that they didn't have the time to listen to other people's experiences. One of the truly daunting factors which is in play when you try to work out whether or not you have the aptitude for running your own business is the retrospective rationale put forward by those who have succeeded. In researching this book, we found that one of the few things common to virtually all people who set up and run their own business is that they have what could be dubbed a personal legend explaining their success. That personal legend usually incorporates a clear dream, which is portrayed as having been present, like the banner with a strange device, Excelsior, from very early on. The legend also includes a great sensitivity to the market, a keen grasp of strategy, a clear capacity to set goals and manage time, and a native but refined ability to solve problems. The successful owner/operator (probably for precisely the reasons they *are* successful) tends to edit out of the legend elements of the storyline which show personal inadequacies, other than those which are endearing and forgivable. This is particularly the case when there is a chance that they will be quoted by name and company in print. Very few of them are even aware that they have shaped a story which coincidentally qualifies them for the hero role by attributing to them skills and traits which they may not have had at the time, but which they have developed in the years since they founded their business and now believe that they had all along. One prominent and highly successful entrepreneur has managed to develop a legend for public consumption, which he details frequently at management conferences, while never losing sight of the somewhat different reality.

"I say now that I spotted a niche in the market," he admits, under cover of anonymity. "And that's true. But the thing I spotted the niche in the market for, the thing I invested thousands of pounds in feasibility bloody studies of, bombed out within months. Sure there was a niche in the market." He joins his hands in "here's the church, here's the steeple" fashion. "*Sure* there was. One market. One niche. Nobody supplying this particular product. So I did the research, because that's what I was told

you did. You did the research, and customers—
potential customers, that is—all said 'Yo! Wow! Of
course I will buy this gadget. This gadget will save
me money. Soon as you get the production line
rolling, ship me six of them.' So we did up prototypes
and I would never say this publicly, but I kind of lost
interest at that stage and started foosthering around
with something quite different, because prototypes
mean dorks running around talking comparative
pressures and millimetre tensions and all that crap,
and I just wanted to say 'Look, lads, would you wake
me when this is over, right?' So me and another guy
started to produce this other thing for fun, and then
the first thing got to the production stage and I
discovered that I had done myself out of thousands
of pounds worth of grant money by outsmarting
myself and buying second-hand equipment but we
got it together and had the product in time for
Christmas. Packaging right and everything. Only it
didn't sell."

The story of that Christmas is never told at the
public venues where this man is now produced as a
success story. It is never told because it does not fit
into the logical sequence we're used to hearing,
which goes

Idea + Research + Funding + Quality + Marketing + Timing = Success

This particular entrepreneur had all of those things
in place, and they added up to failure.

"But I couldn't even fail right," he remembers. "I
hadn't that many people working for me, but even

though it was clear by late November that the bloody thing wasn't going to move, I just couldn't bring myself to stop everything and lay off people just before Christmas. So like a total eejit I let the production go on. It was weird. Like a manic version of *Snow White and the Seven Dwarfs*. Hey ho, Hey ho, it's off to work we go, and the product is rolling off the machines and getting packed neatly into its cartons—after Quality Control. Don't forget Quality Control. And the cartons are building up and we're all whistling while we work. Meanwhile, the three of us who know how bad things really are have got this *other* number going and we're selling this quite different service under the same company name in order to get some cash flowing, but we don't want the lads that are making the gadgets to know too much about it in case they add two and two together and realise the gadgets are going down the tubes. I don't even tell my wife that I figure we're going to lose the house in January. I borrow money from the Credit Union and to this day I can't remember the inventive lies I told them. I put cheques in envelopes without signing so that when people rang me to say they couldn't cash them I would get the extra few days and just look like a fool rather than looking like an insolvent. I put cheques addressed to Peter in envelopes addressed to Paul and sent them off for the same reason. I came into the office I shared with my partner in January, grey in the face with lack of sleep and he nearly gave me a stroke because I thought the office was empty and went in, sat down, lit up a fag because I had gone back on them having given them up seven years before, and the next thing this great red-faced lunatic climbs up from under his desk. One minute I'm there on my own, and the next thing Head the Ball is there too, dusting himself off and pretending it's perfectly normal for a company director to be hiding in the well of his desk at ten in the morning. Turns out that the previous two days he had had a lot of hassle with one particular guy we owed money to, and the guy slammed down the phone the previous evening having said he was just going to arrive the following day and stay until he got his money. So I arrive and my briefcase apparently bucketed off the door before I came in and Head the Ball decided I must be your man come to dun him and drops his ass in under his desk. I think he considered staying there, but he knew I probably couldn't afford to go out to lunch and he worked it out that as a result, he might be trapped there the whole day!"

For the first four months of the new year, both men spent a good deal of their time, physically and metaphorically, on the run. Because the directors of the company were also shareholders, there was a sense of impending shared disaster and a commit—ment to collective disaster prevention. None of the executive directors took their salaries. Credit cards were pushed to the limits. Family and personal purchases were postponed. "By April, we were in this really odd situation," the entrepreneur recalls. "We knew that the product we had set up to produce, let's call it the Whatsit, was not going to earn its keep. Was not going to sell. Was a lemon. Was ready to join a long line of unsaleable product lines that goes right back to the Edsel car. But although we had slowed down production, on the basis that after Christmas, demand would be a bit soft, we couldn't really stop production altogether, because that would mean that the state-sponsored fellas'd start looking for their grants back, and the creditors would start yelling for receivers or worse and the banks'd foreclose and the impact, in an area like this, would be horrendous. It would certainly ensure that the other service we were beginning to sell would die on the vine; if we failed with the Whatsit, we'd have no credibility to do the other thing."

The families of the shareholders involved were puzzled by the fact that the three Daddys and one Mammy Directors were all, as far as the public eye could see, the driving forces behind a plant that was employing more than a dozen people, and yet a request from a student for the money to bankroll an educational trip to Wales seemed to throw parents into spasm.

"We kept having informal board meetings and it was half-way between funny and tragic. There were four of us. Two of us always made with the comforting clichés, you know—Let's not throw out the baby with the bathwater, let's just hang in there, there'll be light at the end of the tunnel, these are the circumstances that separate the men from the boys, etc etc etc. The other two—the solicitor and the accountant—just sat there grey in the face most of the time, because they kept allowing themselves to be persuaded not to cave in when every bit of their training and discipline said that the proper thing to have done was cave in long ago, and they knew they were getting in deeper and deeper."

One stroke of good luck was when a member of the four happened upon a reference to a failed company in a book he was reading. The book was about new companies which had gone down the tubes, and the director was finding the accounts of other people's mistakes oddly therapeutic.

"He came in one morning and he was telling us this story from the book about a company that had missed out on a crucial order because they couldn't produce their product in enough volume. I wasn't half listening to him, but something he said attracted my attention and I made him go back over it."

The story was of a company which had lucked into an order from a huge cereal manufacturer, which wanted to include a freebie in their boxes of breakfast food. The order was of make-or-break importance to the company, which was poised to make it into the big time or retreat. In the event, retreat was what happened, because the cereal maker needed enormous guaranteed volumes of the product over a relatively short period of time, and the other company, faced with the need effectively to tool up a couple more plants to meet this demand, backed off and rationalised.

"I was listening to this sad scéal and I swear to God it was like in the cartoons where a light bulb comes on over someone's head; *idea!* Here we were, up to our shagging armpits in cartons of Whatsits, going nowhere. Why wouldn't we do a deal with a cereal company to give one of them away in each packet?"

The other directors told him why. If the thing hadn't sold in the shops, why should the cereal company be interested? Small pause for thought. "I said to them that we could portray the few months in the shops as a pilot, as a test-run, and say that the shops that had taken it were really happy with it— we could always get a couple of friendly retailers, or retailers who were genuinely sorry for us, to say nice things about the Whatsit. Plus we had all the initial research we had done, that had got us into the mess in the first place. That research indicated that people really liked the idea of the Whatsit and saw it as a very useful *family* product. Plus we could point out to the cereal company that we had been building up stores of the product and *not* putting it into the shops in order to give exclusivity to whoever wanted to carry it as a freebie. Plus, plus, plus...Don't remind me. By the end of the day, we had re-written history better than Stalin ever did and we had a proposal damn nearly finished for sending to the cereal company."

It was not an easy sale, but the cereal company eventually committed itself and took the product at a discount rate which was little better than break-even for the Whatsit makers. Existing stocks were cleared and production justified for another three months.

"We got good publicity out of the deal, and that allowed us to really build up on the other thing. Cashflow improved and our bankers began to sit back a bit in their chairs. We began to pay off the people we owed, bit by bit. Sometimes we even got so flush with money that we paid *ourselves*."

At the end of the first financial year, the company made a loss which was not enormously larger than had been predicted. What the figures did not fully reveal, however, was that the loss on the key product had been of unplanned monstrosity, that this had been mitigated by providing a service which had never featured in the corporate plans, and that shoving the Whatsit into cereal boxes effectively wrote *finis* to its long-term future as a retail item.

"We were friends and we were survivors and we had a sense of humour," is how the Managing Director now sums up the story. "It took us three years to break into profit, and when we did, it was very mild profit. We built up a reputation and quietly buried the Whatsit. Today, our name is known and we are regarded as a good solid business, so we don't ever tell people outside our own circle the full story. The odd thing is that among ourselves, we get much more gas out of telling the stories of the company bad times than we do out of telling the stories of the big sales we've made subsequently. There's nothing like bad times for welding a group of people together."

That particular entrepreneur publicly tells only a tightly edited version of his corporate story, partly because of the damage the true story might still do his company image, and partly because he would not wish other budding entrepreneurs to follow his example. In this, he is rare. The average successful entrepreneur is convinced that he/she has found the way, the truth and the light, and that his/her experience is applicable to every other entrepreneur.

Not true. Entrepreneurs come in every shape and size and the methodology which works for one person may be quite wrong for another person. But if you want to examine the elements of your own suitability to be your own boss and set up your own successful business, then hear this:

Entrepreneurs Need No Specific Educational Background

One of Australia's biggest business empires was (it is said) started by a man who called his company IXL, because he wanted the name to express a personal claim ("I excel") but was illiterate, and spelled it the way it sounded. Many entrepreneurs are dropouts from school or college. But when a successful entrepreneur is under-educated, you can bet your life on two things:

- He will know what he doesn't know

  and

- When he needs information or skill that he doesn't have in his personal armoury, he will unselfconsciously go out and either learn it or find someone else who already has it and can put it to use on the entrepreneur's behalf.

Entrepreneurs Need to Be Flexible

We have a favourite example of the Inflexible Man. We even call him that among ourselves, which is dodgy, because he would be annoyed by the description. He shouldn't be, because his inflexibility is perfect for the job he is in. If he ever decides to go into business on his own, though, he's in dead trouble. The Inflexible Man was into Time Management before it became a dogma. He gets up at 6 and goes for a run. By 7.30 he has been home, showered and eaten one slice of wholemeal toast with marmalade, no butter and a cup of decaffeinated coffee. By 8.30 he is in his office with a copy of the *Irish Times*. A ten-minute delay at this time of the morning throws him, because his parking place is not assured later than 8.25.

We had lunch recently with the Inflexible Man and we managed to put him off his stroke before lunchtime ever arrived, by telephoning him mid-morning to change the restaurant. "You like seafood, and we've just been told that there's this very good new seafood place halfway between you and us," we explained. "Oh," he said unenthusiastically. "Oh, all right." As it turned out, he liked the new place. Not only was the food good, but the place to which we had originally intended to bring our custom had annoyed him the last time he was there by not accepting a particular credit card. "I have others, of course," he said. "But I like to keep all entertainment expenses on one." We nodded in sympathy, if not empathy. Empathy we couldn't bring to the equation because our choice of credit card is always dictated by a mental disaster scale which indicates that while Card A will see us right for a cup of coffee and a sanger, Card B is in such rag order that the restaurateur, on checking with the credit information people, is likely to bring it back to the table and break it over his knee like a deserter's sword.

Our Inflexible Man, meanwhile, was showing us a new electronic memo system he had bought, which allowed him to keep all sorts of data (literally) close to his chest. He had inputted that very morning, he told us, the holiday plans for all employees within his department, right down to the secretaries. One of us got quietly shirty at this point, having come from the secretarial ranks herself and taking a dim view of the placement of secretaries at the lowest rung on the corporate totem pole. Our Inflexible Friend, however, didn't notice her temporary withdrawal, because he was so concerned about the introduction of flex-time to his organisation. This was new and different and would change the way the place operated, he told us, adding, fairmindedly, that even if he had reservations about it, the majority of the employees were totally enthused about how it was working.

This man is an important if not vital executive within a large business. He is conscientious, highly intelligent, caring, hardworking, generous and considerate. He is liked by those above him and by those who work for him. But he should stay where he is. He simply does not have the flexibility to be his own boss or to grow a business from scratch. He is like an ocean liner. He cannot turn instantly left or right in response to an opportunity or threat. By the time the ship has actually changed direction, it will have steamed on and covered several nautical miles following the course it was already on. People who are their own bosses in start-up companies need to have a flexibility of mind which allows them to improvise unorthodox solutions to emerging problems. They are direction-setters, not categorisers. They are concerned with reaching an objective, rather than getting uptight because all the spark plugs do not match.

Entrepreneurs Need to be Persistent

According to Paul Hawken, who, in the 1970's founded America's largest distributor of natural foods, later set up and still runs a mail-order garden tool company, and has participated in a major TV series on setting up and growing businesses, persistence is an underestimated and often mis–interpreted essential.

"From the day you start your company until the day you close it, sell out, or retire, being in business will be one long, continuing effort," Hawken maintains. "Persistence is applying yourself doggedly and relentlessly to the daily tasks at hand, knowing there are no shortcuts. However, persistence does not require being bullheaded or overly aggressive. It does not require a Type A personality. Business persistence is a gentler quality, almost equine in its steadiness. We may lose sight of this because the business press is often guilty of describing companies and industries in terms of campaigns, victories, retaliations and humbling defeats: business as war games, with the captains of industry setting strategy in their Lear jets. Journalists and their readers want the complexity of the commercial world reduced to this charade of someone winning, someone losing. Such journalism belies the more pedestrian qualities that make companies winners, and foremost among these is persistence: never quitting, always trying, always working at the next problem."

(Paul Hawken, *Growing a Business*, 1987)

Entrepreneurs Don't have to Have Come Up through the Ranks in the Skill on Which They Plan to Build a Business

They don't have to. But it does help, when you're looking for money from a bank or a grant from a state-sponsored body, to have your proposal backed by years of experience working for someone else in the same area. The institution which is putting money behind you has the comfort of believing that you know what you're doing. (It does not, of course, follow that just because you have been doing something for eons, you are, ipso facto, well positioned to be your own boss doing that particular thing. Huxley said that experience is not what happens to you, but what you *do* with what happens to you, and there are many people who have a history of participation in a particular industry, but no resultant wisdom applicable to their own business.)

Supporting the preference of banks and other institutions for people who have prior experience in the business they plan to run is a substantive body of experience indicating that the wish is *not* father to the deed, and that a major leap from an area where you know what you're doing to an area about which you only have hopes and dreams does not always pay off. Readers of biographies have noted that a common factor recurring with deadly repetitiveness is the desire of a man or woman, ostentatiously successful in one sphere of life, to move into a quite different sphere and be successful there. (Jeffrey Archer's hunger to be more than a bestselling novelist, expressed by tinkering with the works at the Conservative party, is just one recent example of this. It works the other way, too. Writers are constantly irritated by people who are successful as politicians, industrialists, scientists, doctors or musicians, but who "really just want to write"—the implication being that any fool can write. What is truly irritating about this is that many of them then turn around and do it.)

All of which should not discourage you from trying it, if you want to make a radical shift in career. There are enough precedents around to encourage you. Take Michael O'Kelly, for instance. He was a chef and by his own reckoning, a good chef.

"I started in 1976 and finished around 1983. I did my training in the Burlington Hotel for five years and after that I went to America where I worked as a chef in Philadelphia. I also worked in Parkes Hotel, The Granary Restaurant, The Lobster Pot— I went through a few. Freelancing at that time? No. After they took away the businessman's expense account which was tax deductible, a lot of restaurants and hotels like the Hibernian closed. The people weren't spending the big bucks, therefore the wages didn't go up. In 1981 I was earning more than a chef is earning today as Head Chef in a hotel. There's no money increase in the business. There are so many chefs and there's not enough jobs. I wasn't making any money and that's why I moved into working for myself."

He didn't go straight into construction, starting off with painting and decorating. "I knew a bit about what I was doing before I set up. While I was cheffing I did jobs for relatives and friends. I started on a nixer basis. I got to like working for myself. You make your own hours but you're a harder taskmaster than an employer would be because you answer to yourself and you're pushing yourself harder. The satisfaction at the end of the week is much better. I'm a perfectionist. I look for perfection in my work. It speaks for itself. If you don't do a good job you don't get any more work." Before long he had enough business, delivered by word of mouth reference, to make it clear he could be a successful building contractor. Even if he made errors along the way as he learned the financial ropes.

"Yes, I did make an odd mistake in the pricing of a job, but you learn from your mistakes. You might do a job without checking for material prices, thinking that you knew them, but when you went to get the material prices, they had gone up a tremendous amount. At the early stages of your career, your business, you make a few mistakes. You can't make many because you'll be wiped out. It never crossed my mind to be wiped out because if there had been a problem I could go cheffing, driving, painting and decorating."

"Who taught me what I know? Tricky question. I learned from just thinking about the job before doing it plus asking qualified people how the job is done or getting people in to do the job, watching them closely, listen, taking it all in so that the next time I could do it."

Today he runs two operations—Kelly Kitchens and Michael O'Kelly Construction, and has a half year's work booked at any one time. Almost ten years have elapsed since he abandoned cooking food for a living and moved into construction and he never regrets the radical change.

"I never miss cheffing. It's a job where you're behind the scenes. When the people get their meal, they thank the waiter. The person who put the food on the plate nicely decorated, nicely cooked, nicely sauced is the man in white in the back who never really gets thanks."

Entrepreneurs Need to be Eclectic

Some years ago, one of the writers of this book was running a six-month training course for young graduates who wanted to set up their own businesses. One of the trainees was a bright young woman whose application to the tasks set for her was frighteningly intense. But it was a fantastically promiscuous intensity. She fastened on every business principle which surfaced in class and incorporated it into her personal plan. The result of this was an approach clogged in detail and, like the road to hell, paved with good intentions, all of which had the best of the popular authorities behind them.

She seemed to feel that if one New Year resolution was a good thing, then twenty good year resolutions had to be twenty times better, and she was difficult to shift, until the fat trainee put her finger on the problem one day in discussion.

"I've been fat since I was fourteen," this twenty-two year-old announced. "I have been fat, really fat and outrageously fat. Up and down. Yo-Yo weight losses and gains. Come to my house, you'll find every diet book ever written, lined up in the order they appeared. *The Grapefruit Diet. The Pineapple Diet. The Mayo Clinic Diet. The Scarsdale Diet. The F-Plan Diet. The T-Plan Diet. The Oat Bran Diet.*"

The rest of the trainees looked at her in some puzzlement, because of all this seemed something of a non sequitur. "I'm still fat," the girl said, indisputably. "And that's bad enough. But if I had tried all of those diets all together at the one time, I'd be dead, that's what I'd be. And that," she said, turning to her over-conscientious fellow student, "is effectively what you're doing. You're applying every available good business tip to your business and it isn't going to work. You have to know what you're going to do and then select from all the wisdom out there the bits that will help you rather than just weigh you down or cause you to have unnecessary hidden agendas or standards to meet. Nobody's watching. Nobody has a hidden list of things you could lose points by not doing. Just get on with it, OK?"

The observation was deadly accurate. The point was well made. It would be very satisfactory to be able to report that her fellow trainee learned a valuable lesson and went on to become a millionaire. In fact, the friend learned no lesson and eventually ended up as Personal Assistant to an entrepreneur, where her attention to detail served her and the new business very well. Eclecticism—the knack of selecting from different schools of thought, the philosophical smørgasbord a new business needs— she could never learn. Owner/operators, people who are their own bosses, are nearly always as eclectic as magpies when it comes to their reading of business books or attendance at business courses.

Entrepreneurs Are Good Decision-Makers Rather Than Great Risk-Takers

The portrayal of the typical entrepreneur as a born risk-taker is not only inaccurate, but very misleading. Many of yesterday's apparent risk-takers did not put themselves out on a limb because they wanted to or because they had any natural tendency towards risk-taking. On the contrary, they had an understanding of their product and its market, which meant that what they did was no great leap in the dark for them. Because it might not have been done before, it now seems to have been major league risk-taking, but the entrepreneur at the time had very little sense of adrenalin-spurting terror. Instead, they were concentrating on making all of the bits work, getting the costs right and persuading retailers to take their product or stock their wares. It is no accident that one of Britain's best known entrepreneurs, Richard Branson, confines his personal risk-taking to two weeks a year. When he set up Virgin, the airline, with its reduced service and reduced cost to match, he minimised every aspect of the risk he could by controlling the number of aircraft involved and handling the financing in such a way that he was not going to be weighted down the way the larger airlines are. Branson has started 150 companies, but the overwhelming majority of those companies have been sensible responses to emerging demands or preferences Branson or his lieutenants were clued-in enough to spot. When he wants to push his risk button he does it in the course of two intensive "holiday" weeks, during which he will try to set a speed record, balloon across the Atlantic or reach Mars on a skateboard. Not only is this leisure activity intrinsically risky, but he makes it more so by his inability to pull himself away from the demands of his work in order to do advance training to get himself to the level of physical fitness appropriate for the holiday venture, wherever that holiday venture is. Not unexpectedly, he has as many disasters as he has successes—the dunking in the sea off Donegal with his balloon is just one of them. But all the smiling recklessness conveyed by newspaper pictures of Branson should not distract from the facts of the case; he expresses his fondness for risk-taking in his leisure pastimes, not in his business.

According to those who have worked closely with embryonic entrepreneurs over the past decade, it is not risk-taking but decision-taking which distinguishes the successful entrepreneur. The man or woman who is going to make a go of the business venture they're tackling will take no gratuitous risks, but they won't waste enormous bundles of time playing the "on the one hand, but on the other hand" game. At a certain point, they recognise that they cannot control all of the variables in the choice, so they say to themselves, "OK, I may be wrong, but I'm not going to waste any more time on it, I'm going to go for this side of the equation." True entrepreneurs also seem to have an instinct for cutting off the research phase at just the right time. Trainers who work with people who want to start their own business often note that a couple of people on the course have an excessive fondness for the research phase of a project. They will diligently gather information, painstakingly correlate what they have learned, and juxtapose one possibility against another with maximum punctilio. They just don't want to be moved past this stage. When someone suggests to them that they really ought to get a move on, they will say, with gentle reproof implicit in the tone of their voice, that it is unwise to make a judgement which could affect you for the rest of your life without having all of the requisite information at your disposal. More hurry, less speed, they will quote, and while you are thinking up your answer to that, they're gone because they have another appointment with another source of information which may be subtly different to everything they've received so far.

Getting stuck in the research phase is not peculiar to failed entrepreneurs. Academia houses a fair number of students who never complete a thesis because there is just this one extra source they must locate, just one extra reference they need to tie down. It is a way of being busy but not productive, and the person who seriously wants to be their own boss must be aware of it and avoid it like the plague. We're not saying that you should become a hell-with-the-consequences mindless risk-taker. We are saying that *you* are setting out to be the boss of a business, so you had better start by being a boss of the research process and of the timescale of set up. Remember that other observation by the man who thought up the Peter Principle: If you can't decide where you're going, there's a good chance you'll end up somewhere else.

One other point. When you talk to your bank manager or to the IDA (see pages 99 to 125) delay the risk-taking talk. They're not interested. Keep it for later, when you're a success and someone wants to profile you for a national newspaper or a magazine. *Then* bring out all the human interest yarns about how you realised you would have to sell your children's toys on street corners if this didn't work out, about how the ESB cut off your electricity but you went ahead by candle-light, about how great big hairy things began to haunt your dreams, but you gritted your remaining teeth and faced them hairies down.

Entrepreneurs Are Good Communicators

No, not necessarily good public speakers. No, not necessarily good at being interviewed on radio or television. No, not necessarily chatty people. But they can sum up their business in one sentence. They can tell you clearly what differentiates their business from that of their competitors. They can brief people who work for them so that there is no confusion about what is to be done or the time available within which to do it. They can write a note that someone can understand, make a phone call that activates a process. Above all, they can listen so that they don't miss out on the invaluable information casually transmitted every day by customers, friends, employees and people in conversations overheard at bus stops.

Entrepreneurs Are Rarely Motivated Primarily by Money

Analyse one of any dozen good small businesses and you find that the boss could have done financially much better much sooner by applying the same level of energy and talent as an employee within a large company. Money is usually an objective that entrepreneurs mention, but it is rarely the most important one.

Entrepreneurs Are Not Ruled by Precedent

What we mean here is that good boss/entrepreneurs are not ruled by precedents they have established themselves, for the sad truth is that someone who starts up a business and has a success may then get calcified in their thinking, and if they start up a second business, may drive it into the ground by applying the same methods which made the first one a whiz. On a large scale, the prototype of this kind of failure is Frank Lorenzo, an American business golden boy who managed, in three short years, to ground and effectively bankrupt an airline. Lorenzo had started his climb as a consultant, telling other companies how to run their operations, and was called in by the Chase Manhattan Bank in 1971 to work out a way to save a small, troubled airline called Texas International Airlines. Lorenzo came up with a plan which involved himself at the helm. He then arrived into the company, cut wages and benefits to workers, faced into a strike and brought in replacement labour. Because of the circumstances of the time, which included a pact among the airlines that if one of their number was closed down by a strike, the other airlines would pay the one that was grounded considerable fees on the basis that they were benefitting from business the strike-bound carrier was losing, Lorenzo beat the unions into submission and was seen as a fashionable exemplar of the tough boss who creates that marvellous cliché of the Eighties, "a lean fighting machine." Lorenzo progressed upward so fast you couldn't see his heels for smoke, first with Continental and then with Eastern Airlines falling into his maw. Like a child who has learned a lesson too literally, Lorenzo applied precisely the same principles to Eastern, and could not seem to budge when it became clear to everybody that it wasn't working. The strike at Eastern grounded airplanes, but for the first time ever it also put pilots alongside the bulk of the airline's workers in a solid determination not to be beaten by this man, even, as transpired, if many of the pilots ended up on the bottom salary rung at other airlines, having lost a fortune rather than, as they saw it, sacrifice safety and self-respect to Lorenzo's ruthless search for profit. On April 18, 1990, New York's Bankruptcy Court ruled that he was no longer fit to run Eastern Airlines. One imagines that Lorenzo is still puzzled by the fact that what worked once did not work at all in a different context. He was a man crippled by his own precedent.

Entrepreneurs Don't Buy the Image Myth

Publicity can be useful to a business, and free publicity is even better than publicity you have to pay for. (See page 227). But sometimes, publicity is a two-edged sword for the entrepreneur.

Example. When this book was being written, our press cuttings service one week delivered a most impressive half page feature about the plans of a business then in its fourth year of operation. The picture was of the Founder/Boss, shirt-sleeved and dynamic at his desk. The story was of a buyout which had been declined, a development which was only sketchily outlined, and of a venture which had been a breakthrough. How interesting, we thought, and we began to investigate. Within days, we had been told by people operating within the dynamic shirt-sleever's business sector that the breakthrough venture had cost the company a fortune, that not selling out when the going was good had been a mistake of gigantic proportions, and that the sketched development was about as likely as snow in August. A couple of months later, much smaller pieces began to appear in business pages about a reorganisation of this particular business. For "reorganisation" read "break up and sell-off of assets." The Boss of this particular promising venture had placed too much emphasis on achieving good coverage for himself and his business, and had believed what he then read in the papers—with fatal consequences.

By contrast, one of the most flourishing entrepreneurs in Ireland has no public image at all. He owns or part-owns several companies and is quite happy if one of their executives wants to get his or her picture taken and be interpreted as the guiding light behind its triumph. He neither appears at nor attends management or marketing confer-ences. He does not socialise, collect paintings or sponsor events opened by government ministers or TV personalities.

At some stage recently, he was avoiding having his picture taken for a brochure which was to be used by one of his companies and the PR executive who was working on the project worked up a head of steam trying to persuade him. "We could have you pictured in a way that would really show how go-ahead you are," she told him, drawing in the air with long puce fingernails. "Maybe have you just boarding a private jet to show that…" At this point the Boss and his two fellow directors laughed so much that the PR woman got positively offended, until it was explained to her that he had always had a virulent fear of flying. "But—" she said. But nothing, he retorted. Way back when he was starting up the first of his businesses, an important meeting had been suddenly scheduled in London and there was no way he could get to it without flying. So he set off for Dublin Airport, resolved to be brave, and, turning the corner just north of Collinstown, discovered an airplane sitting crossways in the road in front of him. This had happened when a flight heading to land came down somewhat short of the runway and arrived athwart the Belfast/Dublin road without major injury to passengers. The accident did, however, have a conclusive effect on the entrepreneur, who took one look at the downed plane and went back home swearing he would never set foot on a plane as long as he lived. In the perhaps twenty years since then, he had lived up to that promise, in spite of having multifarious overseas interests. Mostly, he influenced or controlled those interests by phone, telex and delegated executives. If his physical presence was required, he took ferries and trains. But the pictorial representation of his dynamism by having him boarding a jet would certainly have created a certain credibility gap.

Every now and again, a boss begins to behave, within the company or the family, as the publicity suggests he should. Ireland is too small to tolerate this, and a smart aleck employee or spouse will quickly tell The Unorthodox Supremo of the X Business that he should buzz off and produce the Unorthodox Supremo mannerisms somewhere else.

Entrepreneurs Don't Postpone, Don't Make Excuses

Postponement of tasks, particularly of arduous, burdensome tasks, is such a general habit among business people that a complete industry has been built up around it by sharp cookies, not to say main chancers, who get paid to teach you to do things on time and will even supply you with a tailor-made diary system to make sure you keep your notes in unforgettable places. If you are happy to put things off until tomorrow or the day after or next Leap Year, forget being your own boss. Postponers are often excellent people who get every detail right. But they need a driving boss above them who rams a deadline down their neck every time they raise their heads above the parapet.

The truth about excuses is that nobody knows they make them. People turn up at AA meetings and chemical dependency therapy sessions every day of every week and are startled to find that the excuses that have served them well up to now are no longer valid currency. Unfortunately, this is a lesson which has not percolated through to the rest of the population from recovering alcoholics and drug addicts. An excuse never sounds like an excuse to the person giving it. It sounds like a very good reason. But you cannot sell an excuse, and you cannot run a business if you make excuses for your mistakes and failures. Learn from the former and prevent the latter, but outlaw excuses.

Entrepreneurs Are Good Networkers

They make contacts and friends, keep telephone numbers, are not afraid to ask for help and even, under pressure, to specify that it be help free of monetary charge, and they never make an enemy by accident. Getting the business is always more important to an entrepreneur than proving a point or making someone see the error of their ways.

Entrepreneurs Are Happy Workaholics

People in the early stages of becoming their own boss often work eighty-plus hours a week. People who have their own businesses up and running often work much longer than they would have to work in a "normal" job. So are they all exhausted, depressed, physically drained and prey to every floating virus? Short answer: no, they're not. There is a popular idea based on neither history nor medicine nor observation, that people are healthier if they get eight hours sleep a night, do forty hours work per week and devote goodly tranches of planned time to relaxation. In fact, the certified sickness level is often very low among people who work for themselves, because they have less time to notice minor symptoms and no inclination whatever to take them seriously. One executive in a partnership was so amused when she took an ailment to her doctor and received a certificate allowing her time off work that she went straight back to the office—where else? and stuck it to the wall with Blue-tack.

"People who work for other people need certs," she commented. "People who work for themselves need cures."

One writer/doctor who has specialised in psychology has done his best to explode the theory that relaxation=wellbeing. "To relax after hard work is pleasurable only insofar as it is inseparable from the day's activities, the enjoyment that we appear to gain from it springing rather from this source and in fact existing despite the relaxation rather than because of it," maintains Dr Garth Wood, in his book *The Myth of Neurosis, Overcoming the Illness Excuse,* 1986. "It has no lasting intrinsic value of its own. Thus a strenuous day in the steel mill or the office is followed by an unwinding in the hot bath, a relaxing glass of alcohol, a sedentary evening in front of the television. But it is the former and not the latter which contributes to the increase in self-respect that is the only lasting source of gratification. The relaxation panders to our desire for physical comfort rather than to our need for meitonal satisfaction. Relaxation is valuable, necessary and worthwhile for the efficient functioning of our bodies and minds, for our muscles and joints as well as for our psychological well-being, but unlike hard work, it is not intrinsically good for us and should not be sought for its own sake."

People who are born to be their own boss know this instinctively and usually act on it. But they do so despite the well-meaning efforts of their relatives and friends who are convinced that anything over forty hours a week is working too hard, and that working too hard is dangerous for your health.

Entrepreneurs Stay Doing What They're Good at

So this woman decides to set up a hairdressing business, because she has been a hairdresser in the past, and now that the kids are into their teens, she would like to have her own business and put her talents to work. She goes about it in a very organised way, attending update classes to hone her existing skills and make her comfortable with chemicals which were not in use during her earlier career. She gets her savings together, gets advice from her accountant husband, gets a bank loan and finds a premises. A small staff is recruited, and the business moves along nicely. It does not make quite as much money as she had hoped, and it is not quite as much fun as she thought it would be, but very few things in life live up to expectations, so she gets on with the job.

The problem is that she gets on with too many jobs. This woman was an expert in dyeing hair, which is a complicated and delicate operation which can get you sued if you don't do it correctly. What she should have done was specialise personally in that aspect of the business, and build up a core of clients who "swore by her" and would never go to anybody else to get their locks coloured. Instead, she half-taught her two junior people and then wasted time standing over them whenever they were doing a dye job which presented any difficulties at all. Theoretically, she had freed herself up to do other things, but the other things she chose to do were scattered and wasteful of time. "She sticks her nose in everything and makes herself overworked by doing things anyone else could do," one of her staff mutters resentfully. "She sweeps the floor, she answers the phone, she takes the cash—you name it, she does it. I could be setting a woman's hair and she'll come over and ask the customer does she want coffee. Now I may have asked the customer that and been refused, but the customer, because the boss asks her, will say yes, and then she has to go off with a martyred puss on her to make coffee and it's written all over her that this is beneath her, which it is, but that she has to do it because you can't rely on the hired help. This job suits me well enough because of the location, but there's a high staff turnover here because people get fed up of her running around like a blue-arsed fly doing everything and achieving nothing."

Remember, just because you started the business doesn't mean you have to do everything. Especially when by doing everything you do nothing really well.

4

Where to Get Advice and Help

Being your own boss is easier in Ireland than in
many other countries because of the wealth of advice
which is available, often within a short distance
from wherever you are based. Several state-
sponsored bodies will provide, free of charge, advice
which is rooted in the Irish experience, informed by
an understanding of the changing European market,
and aware of international industrial trends. Play
your cards right and you may also win yourself some
grant money to ease the path to owning your own
business.

But, before you start knocking officially on the
door of the IDA, Údarás na Gaeltachta, Shannon
Development, CTT or any of the other state-
sponsored bodies set up to assist industry, do a bit
of preliminary unofficial knocking first, and add it
to a bit of benign industrial espionage. Knocking
unofficially on doors means wandering in to the
headquarters of whatever is your chosen state-
sponsored body and taking away any free pieces of
paper the receptionist can find you. (IDA has what
they call One-Stop-Shops throughout the country
where you find a mine of information on the services

they provide and what's available elsewhere.) Try early to mid-morning, wait until the receptionist is unhassled, and then ask all the stupid questions you can, and have a notebook ready for the names she gives you when she tells you she doesn't have the answer to that particular question, but that Joe Bloggs up in Whereupon Division would be your only man. Take away brochures, newsletters and information sheets. Go home and have a good read. You will first of all find categories of business about which you never knew, and you will find that some of those categories do much better, when they go to battle with our tax system or our grant aid rulebooks, than do others. (There is one scheme called the Business Expansion Scheme, about which more later, which causes quite sensible people to do the most extraordinary contortions in an effort to prove to the Revenue Commissioners that they fit into the BES specifications).

You will also encounter overlap. First time around, you get this wonderful impression that the IDA is going to give you a grant, and FÁS is going to give you a grant, and if you *labhair Gaeilge leo go flúirseach agus go líof*a, maybe you could even con Údarás na Gaeltachta into giving you a grant, too. Then reality breaks out and you discover that if the IDA gives you a grant to cover training, this relates to what FÁS will do for you and if you have any notions of getting the same money out of both bodies, it'll be goodnight from him and goodnight from the other lot, too. (Or *slán leat* if it's the Údarás.)

Once you have gone through the brochures, it's industrial espionage time. It is now that you've got to get the word on the street, the experience, bitter or productive, of those who have been down this road before you. Oh, we hear you cry, nobody would tell me about their private business. Correct. Nobody will tell you what they owe the bank or how much profit they make on a particular product or what they pay their Uncle James for looking after the electrics. But most people in business are startlingly open with novice entrepreneurs (not to mention with reporters and people writing books) when they genuinely believe that sharing their experience can be of some use to a newcomer. If the newcomer intends to set up in direct competition to the existing tycoon, then that's a whole 'nother ballgame. Generally, though, if you put the word out that you'd like to pick the brains of someone who's already got an IDA grant to find out precisely how the thing worked out, what it really cost and what it achieved, then one person will tell another person. Before you know it, you're getting the down-and-dirty information which will help kick meaning into those elegant brochures which, of necessity, are so generalised in their prose that a minute and personally applicable understanding of what they have to offer is difficult to come by. If you get to talk to a business person who has made good use of state-sponsored services, don't just ask what happened, ask how the person you're talking to made it happen. What are the hints they could give you on establishing the most fruitful relationship with the state-sponsored body which is most relevant to your business?

Finally, just before you go, put one more query to them. "Is there anything I should have asked you that I've missed out on?" This question heads off at the pass the shrug your informant may give after you've left the building, and the mutter "She never asked about X. Maybe she doesn't know about it. Maybe she's just dumb. Anyway, not my job to do her homework for her."

Having asked all of the questions, and made all of the notes (because memories are not as good as we'd like to kid ourselves they are) the next step is to make a list of what exactly you need to know from the state-sponsored body you want to attack first. With the list in your hand, telephone them, and ask the telephonist for help. You have this problem—outline it in a couple of sentences—and you haven't a clue who you should be talking to. Oh, it should be X Department? Great. Now, can she put you through to someone there, but maybe she'd give you a name, first? Names, at this point of the game, are important. When you are doing research into an area the shape of which is being established only gradually as you proceed, you will find that you complete a phone call or a face-to-face information-seeking encounter only to find, hours or days later, that a pivotal bit of enlightenment is still missing and that you have to go back. If you have not established a name relationship, then you face the teeth-grinding irritation of going through the whole spiel all over again to a total stranger who is less than motivated, because, after all, they know they are your second choice of informant. Get names, and when one of those people finds that he or she is no longer the appropriate person to help you, get that first contact to introduce you to the next person, rather than cutting you loose to start again with a new department.

When you are seeking advice, the place you are likely to start is the **IDA**, which, although it comes to mind first as a mechanism whereby Ireland woos and wins multi-national manufacturers and non-manufacturing investment, takes very seriously its role as a fosterer of local business, particularly small business. In 1989, for example, almost 600 companies in the small business category were helped by the Authority. 450 of those firms actually began operations. That meant that nearly 9,000 new jobs were created. In May, 1990 Kieran McGowan succeeded Padraic White as Managing Director of the IDA and quickly laid emphasis on small firms as the seedbed for the medium and large Irish companies of the future, and stated that a key IDA strategy is to encourage a high level of start-ups and to work closely with small firms that have the capability to grow into bigger ones. Nor does the IDA just want to see acorns grow into big oak trees which keep all their ambitions rooted in Ireland.

"We've got to get an acceleration of the numbers of small companies committed to growth outside this country," says Mr McGowan. "I've put a new team in place to spearhead our activity in business development, because the aim is to more than double the number of substantial internationally-oriented businesses emerging from this sector. We want to see the small business sector produce one hundred £2m-turnover businesses within three years."

Given that, right now, there are only about 150 Irish manufacturing companies with a turnover of more than £5m a year, them's fighting words indicative of an attitude to smaller developing indigenous business more positive than might have been the case a decade or so ago, when the major hopes were hung around the necks of the incoming multi-nationals.

In an effort to put data in behind that more positive attitude, the IDA recently completed a benchmark study against which to measure future developments. Questionnaires circulated among the project officers working with entrepreneurs on behalf of the Small Business Division came back, not posing startling new problems, but with the odd unexpected slant on entrepreneurship, such as the finding that forty-four per cent of new projects came from existing businesses and that only fifty-five per cent of projects involve a lone promoter. Now, obviously, the fact that this study looked only at three hundred individual projects means that there was a certain level of self-selection going on. It may be, for example, that a majority of lone-wolf entrepreneurs don't figure that the IDA with its well-established national brief and public commitment to job creation, is going to be interested in helping Ms Lone Wolf to set up something which will only provide one single job for Ms Lone Wolf who may be currently employed by someone else. Ergo, goes the rationale, there is no point in wasting my time and the IDA's time in seeking help to set up a lone wolf operation. Hence the lack of representation of lone wolf operations in the IDA's listing. Less speculative but just as interesting is the indication that existing companies are setting up discrete projects or separate companies to explore new or different markets, and receiving state help to achieve what *In Search of Excellence* guru Tom Peters defines as "skunkworks": a lively innovative breakaway section within a long-established company which not only allows that company to diversify without threatening its core business, but may also serve as a corporate personnel refresher and morale booster.

The findings of the survey underline that getting a bright idea into shape for the marketplace often requires more than one brain doing the thinking and more than one pocket producing the readies; first results show that forty-five per cent of the projects had at least two promoters. Nor did the bright ideas come to the entrepreneurs, Einstein-fashion, in the form of unsought, unheralded insights cast in colourful moving pictures. On the contrary, fifty per cent of the promoters got the idea for the project through their workplace. This may sound as if there are lots of people out there getting paid by employers to steal ideas from those same employers but in fact what it means is that an employee may spot something that his current employer badly needs to facilitate his production or distribution or marketing, and may decide to set up to meet that need and, incidentally, sell to others. So you have:

- An employee in a publishing house sinking her savings into a computer with typesetting capacity to process text at super fast speed for a division within that publishing house which is going for "instant books," i.e., books on topical events brought out within weeks or even days of the event.

- An employee in a high-tech company who spots that the monitor on her employer's bestselling

PC needs a clip-on attachment to hold text being inputted, and decides to design and manufacture this accessory.

- An employee in a video-production company who realises that good videotape shots of almost anything can be purchased cheaply but that nobody has archived them for easy retrieval so that a production company suddenly needing a shot of the Rock of Cashel can get one within minutes, and who sets up a computerised Video Archive.

The IDA's study showed that most of the people who found their way to the Authority had simply tapped into their own general knowledge, where the organisation is evidently filed as "Useful if I ever want to be my own boss." But what was rated as the most important thing that a promoter got from the IDA? According to the project officers who gathered the information together, of all the bits and pieces the IDA contributed to the projects, finance was not always the most important. Surprise, surprise: market research and other assistance provided by the IDA was often more important than mere money in getting a new business off the ground. This finding comes as no surprise to IDA people, who don't necessarily see themselves as stereotyped grant-disbursers. The IDA men and women know when you're just playing them along in the hope of a grant and that you are convinced that once you get the grant, you can do what you like with it. Remember when you were preparing for your first confession and your mother said you could tell the priest anything, because he's heard bigger and worse sins than yours? Ditto with the IDA. They have been through all of the performances people do when there's cheap money in the offing, and they don't think much of any of those performances.

To help you test out the feasibility of your idea the IDA (or Shannon Development or Údarás) can assist you with a Feasibility Study Grant. They (and CTT if you plan to export) will advise you how to do it and give you up to fifty per cent of an agreed amount of the cost of wages and salaries, expenses, travel and subsistence, consultancy fees and the development of a prototype. (See Eolas page 123). Start-ups and very small firms (one to fifteen people) can get an employment grant for each new job they create. You get half when you first employ the person and the other half six months later (that's provided you're still employing them).

If you have the potential to employ more than fifteen people then you could either get larger employment grants or capital investment grants of up to forty-five per cent of the costs of a site or building or equipment.

The IDA has regional offices spread throughout the country staffed by people who deal specifically with small businesses. Apart from its standard advice, grant and feasibility study approach to small businesses, the IDA has, in recent years, also developed a couple of variations on their generally supportive theme. One is called *Patron*, another, *Mentor*.

The Patron programme was started in 1988 to allow small companies to benefit from the resources of much larger ones. Under the programme, some of Ireland's most successful companies "adopt" a small business, offering to the smaller company the benefit of their general expertise or special skills. No money changes hands. What happens is that the IDA matches up the little company and the big one very carefully, trying hard to ensure that the big company has an expertise which is critical to the success of the new kid on the corporate block, whether that's export marketing, technology transfer or whatever. It's an interesting task, this matching, because the Authority also prefers not to have the companies in the same business because of the possibility of eventual conflict of interest. After that, it's a matter of figuring out the nature of the assistance and the frequency and duration of contact. This is where we get to the "how long is a piece of string?" question, because the nature of the contact is so varied. In some cases, there have been relationships which involved sharing factory space or other facilities.

The Mentor Programme also tries to put high level expertise at the disposal of smaller, newer companies. Under the programme, experienced executives act as part-time counsellors, helping companies to plan their business and offering specific guidance in areas like Marketing, Production, Transport and Distribution or Personnel and Industrial Relations. But does it work? Do small companies actually gain as a result? We put those questions to Brian Doyle, who coordinates the programme.

"When we started the programme in 1988 we thought we'd have about twenty companies. Today we have 215. Many of our companies are doing well and are ready to take the next step but just can't. They need some advice and help. That's where the mentor comes in. Companies will be merrily going along making goods but they won't know if they're making money or not. The mentor will advise them on the installation of a management information system—help them with budgeting and costings. Another very valuable aspect of the programme is when the mentor acts as a listening post in a very lonely area. Running a small company on your own can be very lonely. Having somebody to talk to and share your fears is great. Somebody who's not your bank manager, not your spouse," says Brian Doyle.

Some of what the IDA offers the small business is most apposite when the business is already up and running. Some is most germane to the business in its embryonic phase. Either way, the IDA seeks to be seen as a partner of the small business person.

According to Mike Feeney, Head of Small Business, IDA, what small enterprises need is the right advice, the encouragement to develop an idea, the support to make it work and the finance to get it up and running. "We have the people and the resources to give this help at all stages of development," he says.

Údarás na Gaeltachta, the Gaeltacht development authority, is not just an Irish language version of the IDA deputed to take care of those areas of the country where Irish is the first language or near as dammit the first language. The Údarás has a wider brief and a somewhat different way of disbursing funds. So if you are in one part of the country, you talk first to the IDA regional offices, if you are in another part of the country you talk to Údarás na Gaeltachta—or if you are in the Limerick area (Limerick, Clare, North Tipperary, South-West Offaly) you talk to Shannon Development. If, however, you are in Cork, Dublin, Limerick or Galway, you have an *embarras de richesses* in terms of advice and help available, because in addition to their IDA offices (for addresses see pages 256 to 257) these cities have BICs too.

What, we hear you cry, is a BIC, other than a pen or a cigarette lighter? A **BIC** is a Business Innovation Centre, which, according to the Dublin Business Innovation Centre literature, provides "a comprehensive range of services and support to potential entrepreneurs (and existing small businesses) to help them develop their entrepreneurial and management skills and prepare soundly based business plans." A BIC may also provide start-up companies with seed capital, accommodation and other forms of practical assistance.

At first hearing, it doesn't sound that different from what the IDA is offering. The BIC operation certainly shares with the IDA approach an orientation towards manufacturing, technology and international service, but sets out to be much more selective in the companies it helps and also plans, long-term, to be self-financing. The idea started in the USA and was adapted by the regional policy directors of the European Commission. A network of about sixty Business Innovation Centres is being formed throughout Europe with the support of the commission, with an eye on the economic regeneration of their areas through supporting new businesses which fit into BIC's preferred pattern. BIC management are reluctant to have themselves portrayed as either competing with or overlapping with what the IDA offers.

"That's not an issue at all," says Desmond Fahey, Chief Executive of the Dublin Business Innovation Centre. "In many ways, we complement what the IDA is doing. You might have a small potential entrepreneur going to the IDA and the IDA might say to him 'you need to do a Business Plan and then we'll be able to help you,' but the guy might have no clue as to how to put a business plan together. If he came in to us, it doesn't matter that the thing has no shape to it. He can come in and just be himself and say 'here's where I'm coming from and here's what I have to offer and this is what I'd like to achieve, can you help me to structure it?'It literally might just be a counselling session where we'd say to him, 'OK, the idea you have is good, but recognise that there are fifty-six other companies in that business and if you go into it, you'll last a month and that wouldn't be fair to yourself.' He'll go away and do some thinking and maybe come back to us. We see ourselves as offering additionality to the IDA. It's an absolutely complementary role. We'll take companies that are at too vague or small a stage for the IDA to be able to do anything concrete for them and we'll work with them and when the time is right, then they'll get slotted into the IDA scheme of things. There is a referral process from the IDA to us and from us to the IDA and it's beginning to work very well. We also get referrals from the Chambers of Commerce, educational institutions, banks, FÁS, Irish Goods Council, CTT, Eolas and many private companies who are supporters of the Business Innovation Centre."

The BIC concept is much more hands-on than is typical of the way other support agencies operate. In some cases, where a company has clear potential but is likely to grow at a faster rate than its capital base or its management can support, the local BIC may take an equity stake and use some of its resources to manage the situation.

"I see situations where we literally give companies management for little or no cost, for a time," says Desmond Fahey. "Situations where we have a hands-on situation, say at a time when a company is expanding, moving out of its premises, needs to computerise everything, in danger of overtrading. How long will we stay in that hands on situation? It depends. It's like growing a child. At what point do you set the child out on a busy thoroughfare and say 'you're on your own'?"

Some of the children never make it to that point, and that's inevitable. "I know from my own experience that seed venture capital companies in the United States which invest in ten companies know that seven to eight of those companies don't make the real trip. One of the ten will be a very successful company. The second one of the ten is a medium performer. The next five to six are just hanging in there. Two or three of them just drop out."

112

At the moment, all four of the Business Innovation Centres major on providing a service, free of charge, to help would-be entrepreneurs get their act together and into a shape which will interest banks, the IDA, Shannon Development or Údarás and/or venture capitalists. The Dublin BIC sums up its services thus:

- Practical support for entrepreneurs wishing to engage in start-up activities or to develop the potential of their existing small businesses

- Provision of advice and consultancy in the following areas: business planning, market research and development; local/international technology search and assessment; R&D, technology transfer and protection; legal, commercial and financial matters

- Access to sources of seed and early stage venture capital

- Provision or arrangement of facilities for R&D, shared workspace and incubator units

- Provision of ongoing assistance to projects and ventures during their early development phases

- BIC works closely with other State agencies, professional advisors, higher education establishments and other local organisations.

Once upon a time there was AnCO, the Industrial Training Authority, there was the National Manpower Service and the Youth Employment

Agency. Then came the Labour Service Act 1987, and suddenly all were one. That one is called **FÁS**, (*Foras Áiseanna Saothair*), the Training and Employment Authority.

FÁS has offices throughout the country and is of vital importance to someone setting out to be their own boss. Quite apart from services like helping you recruit staff and organising training grants to cover the inculcation of particular skills in your new employees, FÁS offers Start Your Own Business courses which have a substantial track record, going back to the beginning of the Eighties, when it became apparent that more people wanted to explore the self-employment option, partly because more people were losing jobs. All over the western world at that time there was a new push towards facilitating people who wanted to be self-employed. AnCO started to provide training courses for this kind of trainee in 1979. Within a couple of years, there was an increase in the numbers of young people who were failing to get jobs, and, despite the received wisdom from the international scene that the most productive age group for such courses is the forty-plus grouping, the Industrial Training Authority began to provide such training for people in their twenties, on the basis that if you were bucking a long-established national tradition, shucks, why not swim upstream against an international current, too? The long-established national tradition, of course, being the absence of an entrepreneurial culture favouring self-employment.

"Ireland doesn't have a history of people employing themselves," says Denis Rohan, the man who shaped the Start Your Own Business aspect of the training provided by AnCO and now by FÁS. "We all left school at whatever age and we all applied to the banks, the civil service. Our parents encouraged that. The schools encouraged it. Everything was set up for the permanent, pensionable job. We wanted to create an environment where people would at least look at self-employment as a career equal to the permanent job provided by somebody else. Even though we were under a lot of pressure to deliver jobs right there and then, we took the longer view. We set out to develop an attitude in trainees so that even if the project they had in mind right then didn't work out, they would, when they were thirty-plus, remember what they had learned and how to approach it."

One of the prejudices quickly encountered by those early courses was close to that which holds that you can't teach someone to be a writer; either they have it from birth or they don't. There is a parallel school of thought which says that people are entrepreneurial by nature or they're not. If they are, then the state should not waste money training them or nursing them along, because they'll make it without any training or nursing. If they are not, then there is no point in wasting training and nursing on them. After more than a decade of honing courses aimed at entrepreneurs and monitoring their rates of success and failure, Denis Rohan does not fight with the notion that entrepreneurs are born, not made.

"What you can do is maximise the chances of the person who is an entrepreneur actually to succeed," he says. "Our training brings them to a structured approach. Very little classroom work. Much more work on the business idea. Practical work."

In one sense, FÁS is caught between a rock and a hard place. or a multiplicity of rocks and hard places. Off the record, the other state-sponsored bodies and also the banks will tell you that they recommend entrepreneurs to go through FÁS Start Your Own Business Courses as a way of filtering out the no-hopers before those no-hopers start looking for—or worse still, actually *getting*—state grant money or bank lendings.

The powers that be, on the other hand, want happy numbers; statistics that indicate a majority of those going through training ended up owning their own businesses, because if they didn't, what's the point of putting state money into the training process? Nobody who is employed by a state-sponsored body is going to put hand on heart and admit that the best thing FÁS does for enterprise in Ireland is stymie the non-starters. Indeed, the inevitable pressure on those who are giving the courses comes from the fact that a successful stymie is difficult to sell in FÁS's annual report, and so their bias in selection of trainees must be to favour those who have already done a good deal of the groundwork on their idea and seem to have the odds on their side. In which case, goes the circular argument, they might not have needed training in the first place...

Where FÁS has gone into the affirmative action business is in providing entrepreneur's courses purely for women. Not just making it easier for women to get on a general Start Your Own Business Course but providing a quite separate course for women only. It started as an experiment without much rationale behind it, and was immediately provided with that rationale by the women who were on the first course.

"They said things that amazed us," remembers Denis Rohan. "They said they wouldn't have applied for the course if men were on it. They couldn't identify themselves—as women—as being able to compete, because most of them had been home-makers and had been out of the paid workforce, and they felt that men had the experience of continuous working and that they, the women, wouldn't be competing equally. They also felt that women on the course gave one another great support."

But why would a woman need any different kind of support on a Start Your Own Business Course? Because, said the women, they had low self-esteem. After years at home, they were likely to make ignorant comments in areas like marketing or production and they found it more difficult to bounce back after making a mistake. To which the reflex response may be; well, if they're so damn vulnerable and wimpy, they're never gonna make it out in the hard, tough business world, so why waste training on them? The short answer is; because the end results justify it. FÁS, as a corporate entity, may be reluctant to state it as a major truth, but the fact is that the results of the women's courses in entrepreneurship are consistently better than the results of the men's courses.

117

"I have a theory myself that women, by nature, are better entrepreneurs than men," says Rohan. "Women are good at calculating risks, and they're good at following through to the end. Men in general seem to give up earlier. The other thing is that women are used to budgeting. If they're at home, they're self-employed in a sense anyway, and if they run their houses on a weekly basis or a monthly basis, they know at the end of a certain length of time precisely what the budget has to meet." Another factor contributing to the success of the woman entrepreneur seems to be that they're used to instant and often hostile feedback, from husbands and children in relation to food as chosen and cooked for the family table. So they are often less threatened, out in the real market place, by comment that their product is too expensive or shoddily finished or not deliverable in sufficient volume to meet the purchaser's needs. They can absorb the blow, learn the lesson and move on.

Of the people who have gone to FÁS for training over the past decade, approximately thirty-five per cent have started their own businesses and made a go of it. Or, as the FÁS people say, "passed through the Valley of Death," the Valley of Death being a make-or-break period somewhere between two and three years after set up, when the initial excitement has subsided, the early goodwill orders have slackened and the shine has worn off the novelty of being your own boss. The thirty-five per cent rate is somewhat better than in other countries. Despite the lively enterprise let's-not-talk-failure-here culture of the United States, there is an eighty per cent failure rate in new businesses. Or perhaps the admission of such a high failure rate is attributable, over there, to the fact that failure is not regarded as a blot on someone's copybook. In America, you can fail at something and move on mentally, physically and geographically to something new and very few people ever know you cocked up. In Ireland, failure sits like a tattoo on the forehead.

The judgemental nature of Irish society makes it tough for the entrepreneur whose project gets exterminated, which is why, in researching this book, when we tried to reach people who had started a business and seen it fold within a year or so, we found that many of them had left the country.

"Ireland is too small for failure," one of them told us on a phone link from Australia. "It's not that people have contempt for you. It's just that they *know* you. You go along with your new idea and it's a great idea and they get turned on by it, and then you can see connections being made and they say 'Aren't you the fella that did X or Y' and suddenly it's like they're seeing you through sunglasses. I don't think Australia is any better than Ireland—I haven't bought any of the myths. It's just allowing me to take myself out of the contention for a couple of years at home, do something different, so that when I go back, I won't be the one that failed at something, I'll be the one that had a great success somewhere else and came back home afterwards."

All of which said, if you have decided that training would help you to become one of the thirty-five per cent who survive the Valley of Death, then talk to FÁS about their Start Your Own Business Courses.

They are twenty weeks long, and the people running the course expect you to have an idea of what it is you want to do, not just an attraction to the lifestyle of the self-employed. The course involves a great deal of supervised market research which allows trainees to get a picture of the real as opposed to the hoped-for market for their product or service. After market research comes financing, during which the trainee looks at pricing and costs. A financial plan is developed as a result of that and, assuming the trainee has not lost interest and dropped off along the way, eventually a complete business plan. FÁS courses are open to unemployed people, and you get paid a training allowance, which is just as well, because the course is a tough and fulltime commitment.

(Enthusiasts will quote you Geoff Read, the man who started Ballygowan Water, as "just one" of the course's success stories. Cynics will say if the course is so successful, how come Geoff Read always bubbles to the top as the only example anyone can remember. FÁS people raise resigned eyebrows and say that the country is dotted with one-and two-man or one-and two-woman operations which have started as a result of the course, but that it is up to each and every trainee to grab two handfuls of the skills the state-sponsored body can offer and then go make it on their own.)

Even when you have finished the basic Start your Own Business Course, FÁS may have more to offer you. They run night-time courses for people who are currently employed, who have a business idea and who are not reckless enough to abandon the day job in order to explore the idea. The FÁS night courses offer these people a low-risk method of exploring the realities.The cost of the course, at time of going to press, is £80. It takes three hours one night a week for ten weeks and is run in FÁS training centres throughout the country. Contact your local centre for information.

If you are unemployed and have been getting the dole there is an "Enterprise Programme" that you can apply for from your local FÁS Employment Services Office. The Enterprise Programme gives you an opportunity to develop a business idea through a ten-week business appraisal training programme, technical training if necessary and income support of up to £65 per week.

The one thing stressed by every one of the state-sponsored bodies which assists entrepreneurs is that the Irish market is restrictively small and that attention to international markets is the key to long-term success for many businesses which are based in this country. On the other hand, they admit that for a two-or three-person business, the exigencies of overseas marketing are on such a scale that they may paralyse even the most go-getting entrepreneur. Which is where CTT comes in.

Córas Tráchtála (CTT), The Irish Export Board, say that you should be looking at the export market when you are first preparing your business plan as the Irish market is so very small. Should you decide that you want to explore the possibility of export then CTT's headquarters is the place to be. In their Market Information Centre they have trade directories on who manufactures what and where, sector by sector. They have market information, research reports, mail order catalogues. Textbooks on marketing, design and transport. Specialist periodicals. Access via computer to over sixty data-banks. You name it, CTT has it. This is all what they call "desk research" and they like you a lot if you telephone before you come.

CTT will then tailor-make services to meet your specific needs with the help of their overseas network. CTT jargon calls it a market investigation and what it really does is answer your questions. "What's the market size?" "What am I up against?" "How do I enter the market?" They can then make appointments for you to meet with your potential foreign customer. CTT work closely with the IDA, and the Feasibility Study Programme we talked about earlier (see page 107) will help finance some of your expenses in the research area.

CTT also subsidise marketing trips overseas and attendances at trade fairs by contributing up to fifty per cent of the costs involved up to an agreed maximum amount.

Teagasc, The Agriculture and Food Development Authority, has recently started running courses for farmers who want to diversify from the traditional farming area. Teagasc asked farmers to look at their resources and become more market orientated. A forty-five-cow farm may be able to support one family but when the farmer's son decides to marry and live on the farm also then it will be very difficult for two families to survive on the original income.

Farmers are asked to look at resources they have on the farm like outbuildings that could be turned into holiday homes, land suitable for a golf course or maybe growing trees for other farmers or garden centres. The course costs £200 and runs for twenty-four days over a ten-week period.

If you have a new product or idea, **Eolas**, The Irish Science and Technology Agency, provide an "invention service" whereby they will examine the product and give you advice. You have to pay for this service but may be able to subsidise it through the feasibility study grant.

If you're into fish retailing or processing, then **BIM** (Bord Iascaigh Mhara) is the place to go. They give you technical advice and sometimes even very politely tell you not to do something. Seemingly somebody recently shouted "enough's enough" when somebody said they wanted to get into smoked salmon. BIM will obviously know if the market is being flooded and will let you know that if you do decide to go ahead with your idea you just might not survive.

The **Irish Goods Council** gives marketing help and advice to small manufacturing companies, although they don't actually give you money. They run a marketplace programme with the IDA whereby a marketing graduate is placed in a company. It could be yours. They also organise in-store promotions for groups of Irish manufacturers.

County Development Officers located throughout the country, are a great source of local knowledge. They work closely with IDA's regional offices, Shannon Development, Údarás na Gaeltachta and the Business Innovation Centres. In some parts of the country they can offer grants and very often have land or buildings which would be suitable for small companies.

If you plan to do something in tourism then talk to **Bord Fáilte** as they have various incentives.

Lest you should get the impression that the commercial sector has relinquished the fostering of small businesses to the state sector, let us reassure you that some of the banks and the accountancy firms knock themselves out to provide general advice with no strings attached, often in the form of excellent informational booklets.

In addition, in spite of the fact that all of this help is available without cost to the entrepreneur, there are businesses being set up to service entrepreneurs and get paid for it, too. Former IDA executive Jane Williams played around with a lot of entrepreneurial ideas, including venison farming, before setting up *Commencements* Ltd. in 1988. *Commencements* is what it sounds; a service to start up companies. The firm, which now employs five people, does everything from winning seed capital for client companies to providing hands-on management on a short-term basis. Like the companies she now helps, Jane Williams encountered predictable problems in the early days of *Commencements*.

"There's a lot of scepticism and inertia you've just got to close your mind to, because there's an awful lot of people out there who would very quickly put you down, if you let them get under your skin." One of the put-downs she encountered was "Oh, she has a husband with a cushy job, she doesn't really need to work."

"That doesn't get in my way, however. But curiously, that relates to the other businesses I work with, too; the personality and attitude of the person at the top. I've seen businesses where the culture of the person who started it means it's never going to go anywhere or it'll go somewhere at the beginning but then die because it needs to change and evolve over time." *Commencements* does not just move into a company, analyse its problems and leave a report on paper for the company to use or ignore as the fancy takes it. What they provide is closer to contract management. They implement as well as advise.

Unlike BIC, which if it sees a worthwhile small company stalled at a particular point because of lack of capital, may actually take a stake in that company, Jane Williams' company goes on the hunt to raise venture capital from third parties, having first of all worked out with the growing client company what they believe a stake in their company is worth and what the market in this instance will bear. Bosses of successful small companies are often grossly overconfident or startlingly modest about the worth of their enterprise. Ms Williams sees part of her function as damping down over-confidence and inflating undue modesty. Either way, her company's contribution to another company's development is not just a passing phase.

5

Getting Started

In order to get your business up and running, you
have to take your great idea and apply Kipling's six
questions to it.

> *I keep six honest serving men*
> *(They taught me all I know)*
> *Their names are What and Why and When*
> *And How, Where and Who*
> *I send them over land and sea*
> *I send them East and West*
> *But after they have worked for me*
> *I give them all a rest*
>
> (Rudyard Kipling)

You can call the process by any number of fancy
names. You can call it Advance Risk Management.
Market Research. Corporate Planning. Strategic
Positioning. But ultimately, it's about asking yourself
and other people a lot of questions, so that you
discover any holes in the boat before you get into it
and set out across the business ocean.

Let's start with the "WHAT?" question and apply
it to your idea. You may have a product in mind that
you plan to produce. Put the "WHAT?" question

beside that product and it breaks down into a number of divergent queries:

- *What exactly is your product?*

There are two quite different answers to this. There is the technical answer, which may be something like this:

- **Product**: Disposable nappies

- **Raw Materials**: Recycled tissue imported from the Recycling Co, Finland; Adhesive tape from the Sticky Co, Dublin; Biodegradable plastic sheets from Break-Up Plastics Ltd., Wicklow

- **Age Range**: 4—10 lbs; 11—24 lbs; 25—40 lbs

- **Packaging**: Packs of 10 and 50 in recycled cardboard boxes which can be re-used as toyboxes, etc.

- **Price**: £X for 10, £Y for 50. (Five per cent lower than the cheapest currently on the market.)

- **Manufacturing Process**: Fully automated with capacity for the production of X units per day.

- **Customers**: Aimed at "green" parents who want what's best for baby and the environment at a reasonable price. Will be available through supermarkets and pharmacies.

That's the kind of answer you need if you're going to talk to

- A paper factory who might produce it for you

- The Industrial Development Authority, Shannon Development or Údarás na Gaeltachta

- EOLAS, the Patents Office, the Environmental Protection Agency (if you want the Minister there to launch your product)

- The bank, venture capitalists or potential partners

If you cannot produce this definition of your product, then you probably need to go through more production planning and investigation—so stay with us throughout this chapter—in order to move your product from bright idea stage to real possibility stage.

The second kind of answer you need to be able to give is the one that will make sense to a customer, either an individual customer buying your product off the shelf, or a customer like the chief buyer for a chain of shops which will put your product on their shelves for the final customer to find it. Here, the kind of answer you need to have is one which makes your product instantly understandable and appealing to the buyer and which distinguishes it from its competition.

So the non-technical answer, stressing benefits to the customer rather than features of its production or make-up, might be:

"My product is the first disposable baby's nappy which is completely safe for the environment. It's made of recycled paper and the plastic in it breaks down thirty-six hours after the nappy is taken out of the packaging. It's softer and lighter and safer than any nappy produced up to now and it's cheaper, too. It's even more environmentally friendly than the old cloth nappies because it doesn't need bleach to disinfect it. And it's extra absorbent, which means the wearer doesn't wake up leaking all over his cot every morning."

One of the things that make the "WHAT?" question useful is if you imagine it being asked by a chain-store buyer who has no interest nor enthusiasm nor time. You've got perhaps five minutes to win serious consideration for your product, and you've really got to make it appealing in the first of those five minutes. The buyer is sitting there filled with hostile variations of the "WHAT?" question, because life is simpler for buyers who deal with the big-selling well-established product lines that do not have to be nursed through teething problems. So the buyer's mind is churning up queries like: "Yeah, but what's special about this? What makes it different? Is it just a 'Me, Too'—a variation on a theme? Because if it is, I have the main theme delivered by a big established company that'll have a conniption if I put an imitation beside their product. Has the patent been taken care of, or would we get used by the original supplier?"

So in preparing your initial answer to the "WHAT?" question, you must first of all be vivid, clear and brief, and you must be ready to answer positively all of the negative questions which are asked—*and which may not be asked*. One businessman who took three years longer to get his product into supermarkets than he expected, told us, looking back, that one of the reasons which prevented faster progress, was that he failed to answer the questions that didn't get asked.

"I would go in there and make my pitch, and they would ask a few questions and promise to think about it, and compliment me on my great concept, and I would go out of there on cloud nine," he laughs. "But then, when I tried to move the thing forward, they were never available. Cloud nine rapidly worked back to being Square One, and I couldn't figure it. Eventually I went to one of my appointments with a friend of mine who's a business consultant, whom I had asked to come with me because I had come to the conclusion that I was misreading the situation in some fairly critical way. I introduced my friend as my partner, and he just sat and made notes throughout the meeting. So when it was finished, we came out and got into my car and I was on a high.

'Hey, wasn't that guy very supportive?' I asked my friend and he looked at me in total silence. 'Well, *wasn't* he?' I pushed, and then my friend shrugged. 'You can't bank "supportive," ' he said. 'That guy gave you ten minutes and got you out of his office in the nicest way possible but you know what he ended up doing? He ended up wishing you luck with this great product. He didn't buy it. To hell with "supportive." You wanted an order. You didn't get it. You won't get it as long as you're over on your side of the fence admiring your product and not telling him what it's going to do for him and how easy it's going to be for him to slot it into his range. The fact that he didn't ask you eight negative questions doesn't mean he was thinking positively. He's just a guy who doesn't get into conflict with strangers in whom he has no investment. Why should he spend time asking you negative questions in order to help you get the glitches out of your product to make it fit for his range? Much easier to pat you on the head and say you're a creative genius and more power to you and he hopes you make a million. That costs him nothing. Doesn't even cost him time. You go away, and one of two things are going to happen, as he sees it. Either you're going to fall by the wayside just as most owners of bright ideas do, or you're going to have sense kicked into you by the marketplace, in which case you'll come back to him with something tried and true it's safe for him to opt for.' "

The entrepreneur sat down with his friend and worked out every negative "WHAT" question the buyer might have asked if he had been so minded, and came up with a list of threatening proportions. What was ultimately of most use about that list was not that it improved the sales pitch of the entrepreneur, but that it forced him back to the drawing board on some developmental aspects of the product. "That took time," he admits. "More time than I had banked on, and I very nearly ran out of money. But we solved the problems and ended up with a much better product. Not only that but after I'd done the extra work, I knew precisely what I had on my hands, and I could tell other people in ways that made the thing take off in their minds, too. Up to then, I'd been like the person who's asked what a spiral staircase is, and who immediately begins to do upward corkscrew miming with their index finger!"

The "WHO?" question, in its simplest form, shapes up like this:

• *Who are you?*

The answer, however, is not simple. First of all, the questioner doesn't want a police description by way of answer: "Mary Smyth, 14 Category Park, Bogsend, Main Town. Telephone: 414141." The questioner, if they're the buyer for a store, wants to know what about you or your history justifies them investing money and shelf space and trust in you. If you have a scientific background out of which the product has emerged, that may help. If you have a marketing background, ditto. If you have production experience, then they are likely to feel that they are not committing themselves to a creative amateur, and most chief buyers would rather commit themselves to a skid-row derelict drinking meths than to a creative amateur.

The "WHO?" question, insofar as it invites you to profile yourself, should be answered briefly and positively. Well, of course, we hear you say. What else would I do? The answer is that you might do what many people do when they go for job interviews. They are asked an open question about their career to this point and they explain how they dropped out of college because they didn't really like university life, and they went to work for their uncle, but working for relatives is always a problem, isn't it, so they left and joined the XYZ company, but the boss there was obviously not going to promote them, and so they went to work for the ABC organisation, and that's their current employer and they want to leave ABC because they're not paid enough and there are a lot of personality conflicts, you know? The interviewer makes notes and asks further questions, but the die has been cast halfway through that first answer—and it is a type of answer too often given. Similarly, if the story you are telling to a potential investor or to a department store buyer is that you developed this product because you first of all got made redundant and although you planned to go to work for someone else, they let you down at the last moment, then you begin to reek of failure and the other person in the room just wants you out. No, we are not saying that you should not tell the truth. What we are saying is that you should tell those aspects of the truth which can be useful to you, and cut back on the narrative when it begins to lead towards the conclusion that this product you're trying to flog is a personal last resort.

Another aspect of the "WHO?" question is *"Who's in this with you?"*

If you are all on your own in your company or if you are operating as a sole trader, then this question must be answered with references to your production capacity, to your bank and to bodies like the IDA which may be supporting you.

If you have a limited company in which a bank or other institution has taken a shareholding, then you mention that shareholding, which indicates to the listener that other sceptical people have decided you know what you're doing. If you have a board of directors which includes some eminent figure, then a mention of the eminent figure adds to your credibility. (The fact that entrepreneurs put *éminences grises* on their boards for precisely this reason and that the presence of those eminences doesn't stop the thirty per cent failure rate of new companies, never seems to dent the utility of having a well known name on the letterhead.)

The "WHO?" question was part of the planning of one highly successful service industry which shall be nameless. "I suppose you could say it was cynical," the company owner admits. "I would rather call it realistic. I was setting up something that wasn't an advertising agency, wasn't a PR company, wasn't a training consultancy. It just fitted into the cracks between all of those things and met some of the needs they have difficulty meeting, so I planned to service the needs of that kind of company as well as directly meeting the needs of client companies. If the concept had at that time been well-established and familiar to people then I could have employed any decent professional with a bit of experience under their belt. But the concept was new, so if I sent in an unknown, the potential customer would be trying to work out whether or not this concept was worth buying from this no-name person. There was no way that was going to work. Whoever fronted for this concept had to be already well known, already well regarded, so that people interpreted the service through the person offering it and said 'well it must be good, because so-and-so is such a good operator.'

I paid twice as much for the Managing Director as I might have paid, but if I were to point to one single factor instrumental in putting us into the black within eighteen months, it was the market-place acceptability of my front man."

The answer to the "WHO?" question can either qualify you or disqualify you. It *can*, but it doesn't always happen that way. For example, AMPEX, the video people, were a well established name, a good, solid "WHO," when they developed the VCR or the VTR as they called it. (Video tape-recorder.) But their name was not enough to ensure that the product got out there and sold millions of units. Other factors got in the way, so that when the VCR finally made it big, it made it big for the Japanese. On the other hand, manufacturers who produce computers often talk about "The IBM Factor." The IBM Factor is what runs through a potential buyer's head when he faces making an investment of perhaps a million pounds in a computer system. The person making the choice may be the Managing Director or may be the Data Manager, but either way, if they get it wrong, it is going to put a major crimp in their career. So they listen to the competing computer companies talking about this marvellous hardware which doesn't have a big footprint, and this even more marvellous software which allows the technology to do six wonderful things nobody else's software can achieve, and they think "Yeah, but what happens if this company can't deliver on time, or delivers software with the hiccups still in it? If I go with IBM, I'll be safe. Nobody ever got fired for choosing IBM." The IBM Factor can mean that a product which is developed by a newcomer and which is demonstrably and objectively better than the product turned out by an established company may be rejected because the buyer subjectively feels more secure with the established company.

Many entrepreneurs do not press their empathy button and work out where the potential buyer is. They assume that if you're in charge of, say, buying nappies for a supermarket chain, you are a figure of power and easy authority. Which may be true. But your power and easy authority can dissipate pretty quickly if you make a lot of expensive wrong decisions, so the person coming to you with a new product had better look as if they can handle the project, as opposed to just coming up with fresh product concepts.

The next question on our list is the "HOW?" question. If you are selling an individual product to an individual buyer, the question may take the form of *"How does this thing work?"* This nappy that you have developed may have a new method whereby one applies it to the baby. This has to be explainable to the customer so that it makes instant sense and so that the customer can apply her understanding (and the nappy) immediately. Look at the instructions on any appliance and you will find that ninety per cent of them are so poorly expressed that it is only after you've worked out how to use the thing that the instructions are understandable. Yet very few entrepreneurs spend enough time working out how the product and its uses can be made accessible to its end users. We once watched an inventive genius make a presentation of a new gadget he had developed. He filled the air with technical verbal mosquitoes and the small audience watched and listened, mesmerised and wary. After a while, the woman who was the key decision-maker stood up and approached the table on which the demonstrator had placed his prototype gadget. The presenter lost confidence in his presentation and ground to a halt.

"I always believe," the woman said sweetly, "that if a thing is going to work in the hands of the consumer, that's how it should be demonstrated, don't you?"

The inventor of the gadget nodded in panicky agreement, not knowing what was meant by this.

"OK, then," the crucial decision-maker said briskly. "You stand over there and I'll work the machine. A hands-off demonstration by yourself. Don't touch it. Just tell me what to do."

The inventor nodded and began to talk her through it. He got her to take it out of its packaging and position it squarely on the table. He got her to switch it on. A satisfying hum emanated from the machine and a little red eye twinkled into life at the front. Stimulated by this, the inventor emitted a splurge of technical background information. The critical decision-maker raised a limp (doesn't this guy ever learn?) but indicative (Stop. Do not pass GO) hand, and asked for the next set of instructions. The inventor embarked on their delivery, but began to edge closer to the table to point to the bits he was talking about. Within minutes, his hand was on the machine alongside hers, and he was so involved with what he was doing that he never noticed when she shrugged and stepped back. At the conclusion of the demonstration, the inventor was blissfully content. So, too, was the audience, because it had become completely apparent to them that what was on the table was one man's toy, not a product ready for mediation to a wider public.

The "HOW?" question has a whole lot of ramifications. How is your product going to be physically presented, for example? Professor Magnus Pyke had a trick which underlined the importance of the physical presentation of an item for consumption. He would dye mashed potatoes a particularly virulent navy blue, and then serve them to hungry eaters. The dish was absolutely harmless. It just looked like the Garda Síochána of the mashed spud, and people couldn't eat it. They gagged on the unexpectedness of it. People buy things for how they look, as well as for what the thing can do for them.

The problem is that entrepreneurs have often expended their creative spurt in the development of the product itself, and they think of the packaging as a minor addendum to the process. Not so. The world will beat a path to the door of the man who invents a better mousetrap only if that mousetrap is boxed so attractively that it does everything short of leaping off the shelf and nestling seductively into the buyer's pocket, singing "Hey, big spender, spend a little money on me..."

We came across an example of this some time ago, when consulted by a man who had developed a new board game. Oh, Yawn, we thought as he laid out the dice and the markers. An hour later, he was the one doing the yawning, as we swore at each other because of the hypothetical fortunes we were making and losing. He was used to seeing this happen.

"But I told you it was a great game," he said in puzzled modesty. "Much better than Monopoly or Scrabble." Eventually, we called it quits, shovelled the dice and markers back into their little containers and asked him what packaging he planned. He glowed like a lamp.

"This is as good as the game," he told us, producing a cardboard mock-up of the box he was planning to use. "You know why?"

We shook our heads, intimidated as always by rhetorical questions.

"Because it's so *compact*," he thrilled. "A board game that expands to two and a half square feet on your diningroom table compresses down to a six inch cube. See?"

We saw. We came, we saw and we were anything but conquered.

"You don't like it?" (This question was not rhetorical.) "My wife designed it. She used to be a designer."

It's at times like this that you remember the old psychologist's Learning Sandwich. You don't know the Learning Sandwich? It works like this. You have something pretty awful to tell someone. They have failed their exam. Their house has burned to a crisp and been removed in one mini-skip. Their granny fell down a well. They have bad breath. They are lousy drivers. Their product stinks. That kind of something pretty awful. So to make a Learning Sandwich out of it, you stick the something pretty awful in between two fat positives.

"C'mere till I tell you," you say. "You have a fantastic family, you know that?" (Fat positive.) "Creative, happy, united." (Fat positive continued.) "Now you should know that your granny just fell down the well." (Fast negative.) The extra space this will give you in your house will mean that you won't have to take out the bank loan you were thinking of to fund the attic extension." (Second fat positive).

Now, frankly, we think the Learning Sandwich is a cod. We think you have to be dumb not to peel off the ritual positive at the top and the consolation prize underneath and get to the sulphuric acid in the middle, but this man was a good guy with a lot of potential in his product, so we tried.

"I really go for cubes," one of us said warmly. "Such a satisfying, solid, pleasing shape."

"A six-inch cube makes the product look too small and mean," the second of us slid in, making the insertion of the shiv as fast and quiet as we could. Me Tarzan, you Mac the Knife? AAAhhh...

"But isn't it marvellous that you have the design capacity in-house, so to speak?" finished the first one, her warmth going up by leaps and degrees. The guy looked at us as if we were a tennis table match and unerringly came back to the one in the middle who had said the bad thing.

"Too small and mean?" he asked.

"Yeah. This thing is going to sell, not because people need it, but because people want it. So it's got to be big enough firstly to attract their attention and secondly to make them feel they're getting really good value for an essentially frivolous expenditure. Especially if they're giving it to someone else. A six inch cube, wrapped up, doesn't look that impressive to a ten-year-old who gets it as a gift."

Having said which, several examples of best-selling toys of even smaller cubic dimensions immediately sprang to mind, so we suggested to him that he needed to do some further research, firstly into how potential end-users viewed packaging for board games, and secondly into how that packaging was to be produced. One of us even got inspired enough to propose to him that his in-house designer might be persuaded to do some of the market research into the packaging, our ulterior motive being that it was easier on everybody if she found it out for herself, rather than be told by the consultants (us) or by her husband (him).

In the course of this research, our client came to terms with one of the inescapable realities of Kipling's Six Serving Men; they're not Sole Traders, any of them. They prefer to work as a team, and they relentlessly create business for each other. The "WHAT?" question leads to the "WHO?" or "WHY?" questions, and often one leads you back to a previous problem you thought you had solved.

So in answering the "HOW?" question, our client worked his way back to the "WHO?" question he thought he had previously answered. Because it emerged that no big packaging producer wanted to know about an order of fewer than a hundred thousand boxes of the particular shape he eventually settled for. The packaging companies said that retooling for a smaller order wouldn't be worth their while. Hc then investigated the smaller companies which welcomed him effusively and affirmed that of course they wanted his business. The difficulty was that their diseconomies of scale added 80p to each unit. The entrepreneur could take that off his profit or he could up the price, but his research indicated that he had placed his product just under the price "ceiling"; if he added another fifty pence, consumer resistance would set in. Because our client is a man of flexible and resilient attitude, he then decided that he needed to sell the game on a royalty basis to one of the big game producers, which would be able to produce it in much greater volume. He is currently negotiating with an interested multi-national game producer along those lines.

The "HOW?" question is alive with possibilities:

HOW much are you going to charge for this product or service? More or less than your competitors? If you're planning to charge more, why aren't you more competitively priced and how are you going to justify that to the consumer? If you are charging less than your competitors, is that going to be an advantage or a disadvantage? (Sometimes cheap equals substandard in people's minds). In planning your charges, keep in mind that a regular customer might ask for, wish for or merit a discount, and what happens your sums if twenty-five per cent of what you sell is sold at ten per cent off the official price? Keep in mind things like VAT and insurance, too. And keep in mind that between you and the end customer there may be a retailer/wholesaler/distributor—all of whom have to earn a crust out of the eventual price.

HOW are you going to transport your goods to the market? Some products have to prove themselves worthy of coat-tailing on someone else's distribution system, because setting up an independent method of distribution could not be cost-justified by the new business. For example, a new publisher of specialist books cannot invest in trucks and truckers in order to get her first book into the bookshops, even if she were unwisely to assume that bookshops all around the country would find shelf-space for an offering from a publishing house of which they had no prior working knowledge.

In this instance, the new publisher will probably come to an arrangement with an existing publisher, to have her book carried along with his list. No matter what business you're in, it is important never to confuse the need for wheels to take your product to market with the need to *re-invent* the wheel. If there is a distribution system out there already, take advantage of it. Many distribution companies have responded flexibly to the segmentation of formerly monolithic markets and can serve quite small producers and exporters. There is, for example, a useful thing called "groupage" which operates on shipping lines. What this means is that your six cartons of biodegradable nappies, which would not justify the hire of even a small container on their own, will be taken by a groupage operator and put in a container alongside someone else's six bags of teddy bears and a third exporter's eight bales of fabric. Read your contract with the transporter very carefully. We know of one food producing exporter who lost a huge order because when his product was delivered, it was clearly contaminated. Investigation turned up the kind of confluence of awful possibilities you hope you never have to face. The exporter had chosen the cheapest transport option, on the basis that one container is very much like another container. Although there is some truth in this general statement, the fact was that the container carrying the exporter's food product had seen better days. It now had a rent in its roof measuring eighteen inches in length and in places twelve inches wide. Through said aperture poured rain, which was bad enough. However, because the system was cheap, it involved an overnight stay in a semi-civilised trailer park near a pub which served a vast and less than gainfully employed hinterland. Some of the young male residents of this hinterland, baulked of anything more exciting to do one Saturday night after the public house closed, climbed up onto the container and, individually and severally, urinated through the hole in its roof. When all of this emerged as the cause of the problem, the exporter was at a loss. Not for words, which were in lively and profane supply, but for an understanding of what the transport company's insurance covered, what his own insurance covered and how to apply the small print to the problem, which was not that this particular order had bounced back as unacceptable but that the flagship overseas customer had withdrawn acceptable vendor status from the exporter, which set company development back a year and a half.

- *How will this product meet national or EC regulations?*

There are some small operators who have an excellent product, and if you come across that product in your local shop, amateurishly labelled and clearly defining itself as harmlessly home made and without serious intent, you will wonder why on earth the makers of this splendid item haven't gone into mass production and cleaned up. The answer may well be that when they investigated the national and European legislation and regulations governing the large scale production of such an item, they fainted in coils. Like the weather, there's a lot of regulation about, and you have to abide by those regulations, because if you do not, such is the natural spirit of competitive begrudgery distinguishing humans from all other species that someone will inform the powers-that-be of your lawlessness. In the course of researching this book, we came across a consultancy firm which was part of a chain. Self-operated, but with the advantages of belonging to a nationwide chain. The founder of the business got his sign made up, in expectation of his full accreditation coming through. It said something like this:

SPOONFEEDERS INTERNATIONAL
Proprietor: Jeff Divoh, SISP

SISP stood for Spoonfeeders International Senior Partner, which he was due to become in November, having been a junior partner for three years. Jeff did not want to create a sign describing him as SIJP which would only serve him for five months and then have to be replaced at great cost to his little business, so the sign calling him a senior partner shone out from his street-level building by the end of June. Three competitive members of Spoonfeeders International immediately wrote to the head office protesting this false claim. Head office got on to Jeff. "Tut, tut, Jeff," head office said. "Furthermore, tsk, tsk. Tell you what, Jeff," head office said. "Cover up the Proprietor bit of your sign for a few months and that'll get those other guys off our back, OK?" "OK," said Jeff agreeably, and got thick plastic of a colour to match the background and nailed it up over the premature sign. Two weeks later, head office called back. "Yo, Jeff." "Yo, Head Office, how's she cuttin'?" "Remember the problem with the sign? Now, we know you put up a cover, but it hasn't really solved the problem. Some of your competitors have sent us pictures. Jeff, the pictures certainly do show that you've put a cover up over the claim. The difficulty is that at night, the neon shows through the plastic and you can still read it if you try very hard." (Wild cries of protest from Jeff.) "Yes, Jeff, we know that nobody goes to a business like yours at night. But could you cover it up with another thickness of plastic?"

The "WHICH" question is about differentiating your product or company from the countless numbers of similar products and companies. Your product may do that for you, if it is unusual enough, but a good name helps it along. The classic example of this was a little soft rubbery octopus which attracted the attention of a visitor to Japan. Somewhere between a toy and a digression, this was to be thrown at a window or a mirror, where at first it stuck, then half disengaged, and progressed slowly downwards in a curious clinging gait. Watching its progress was intriguing and flinging it against a shiny surface was addictive. Ken Hakuta decided to order large consignments of this thing and to try selling it in the United States, where he lived. But he had two problems of differentiation. One was that the thing needed a name if it was to become popular by word of mouth, and the other was that it needed to be differentiated from other toys. Hakuta solved the first by calling it the Wacky Wallwalker—"wacky" being an Americanism for "spaced out." The second problem he solved by defining the thing very clearly as a fad. This determined the outlets through which he could sell it and the publicity he would use. The outlets could not include major discount Woolworth type shops, because they would insist on selling the Wallwalker too cheaply for him to make a profit. The publicity could major on unpurchased TV coverage. For the end of newsprogrammes, the Wallwalker slowly and sinuously progressing down a window made a neat novelty and a mildly amusing visual under credits. Because it was a fad, rather than a long-term project with assured annual sales, Hakuta also decided that he could not afford massive overheads. "Most of my staff for a million-dollar business consisted of me and my wife," he writes. "And she was part time. We worked out of our bedroom. At night, we took crates of Wallwalkers into bed and stuffed them into small plastic bags.

Remember, the lower the overhead, the higher the profit ceiling."

Choosing a brand name is not easy, but before you commit yourself to the considerable expense of having packaging produced and printed bearing that name, first of all you must check with the Companies Office to see if someone else has got there before you, and secondly, you must have decided that you are positioning your product as a branded product. These days we take branding for granted. Even coal is branded, even though it used to be sold just as "Polish coal" or as coal from some other country. Now it has its own labels and logos and identities. But the rugged individual assertion of a brand name may not be appropriate for selling into all markets. If you make a christening layette and you want to sell it through the Dunnes Stores chain, they will probably want to put the St Bernard name on it and to have no labels identifying what factory or workshop it came from. Much the same applies to Marks & Spencer, with some exceptions. The balance has to be struck between assured large scale orders over a predictable length of time (if that is what you are being offered) and the smaller more sporadic ordering by other outlets which would have the advantage of allowing your brand name to become widely known. There are manufacturers who have been supplying Marks & Spencer in contented anonymity for more than a decade, and there are manufacturers who forego an entrée to the M&S shelves because it would not help them to establish their corporate presence. There are also manufacturers who answer this variation of the "WHICH?" question ("Which are you going to be, branded goods or generics?") by nailing their colours firmly to the fence and becoming both. Big companies spend trillions on brand support and, if you're small, competing in consumer markets where brands are strong is very difficult. For example, Pampers, Kelloggs, Heinz. If you want to make nappies, cornflakes or beans and sell them branded, you'd need very deep pockets or a very rich uncle. Doing both branded and generics has its problems. One supplier who ran into heavily publicised quality-control problems told us that these problems affected his generic (unbranded or Own Brand goods, like Yellow Packs or Thrift Packs) business worse than it affected his branded business.

"The general public, particularly the kids who were buying the product, don't pay a blind bit of attention to news stories like the ones that hit me," he said. "OK, a few people would stop buying in the short term, but the majority would eventually drift back. But the buyers in the stores who were using the product as a generic or an own brand just went APE! They wanted to pull out of the contract right away and they wanted to pull out for good. If they went, that meant forty per cent of my business was just lopped off overnight, and it was a forty per cent that would take us years to build up in smaller orders from other retailers—smaller orders we were not in the best position to win, because of the publicity about our quality control hassles. You would think that being in both the branded and generic areas would cover you, but in fact it left us more exposed and vulnerable. Hanging in there with our generic customers took years off my life."

Another aspect of the "WHICH?" question is whether a customer wants exclusivity of supply. This can happen with a product, but it can also happen with a service. If, for example, a large financial institution is buying confidential consultancy advice from a new company, they may make it part of the contract that you do not supply a similar service to their competitors. In which case it behoves you to price your service not only to cover what it does for them, but to cover the business you cannot pursue because of the exclusivity dictates of their contract.

The "WHERE?" question carries with it all sorts of problems on the part of the purchaser, including:

- Am I going to have to drive twenty miles to a special technical headquarters every time I want a refill for this thing?

- Am I going to have to leave my office for the service you offer? (Worse still, in some cities, is the possibility of having to go to an unexpected location. Ever wonder why 99.9% of Dublin's advertising agencies are on the south side of the Liffey?)

- Is this (supermarketeer speaking) going to go in the Healthfood Section or in the Cereals section or in the Snackfoods section?

- Is the product going to be sold in Ireland only, or is there an overseas market for it?

- Is it going to be sold in shops, specialist outlets or

by mail order?

- Is the manufacturing going to be done from the same building as the administration?

The "WHEN?" question is one of the most difficult, especially when you are faced with it at an early stage in your company development. There you are in front of a potential client who is very open to what you have to offer, and eventually, they get to the nitty gritty.

- "If I were to order two dozen, how soon could you deliver them?"

The question may be unanswerable. A response like "If someone your size only orders two dozen, then I haven't a prayer of making it, so I'm not going to waste my savings setting up a factory to make your lousy two dozen," may hit the nail on the head but it also hits on the head any subsequent useful contact with that potential client.

Meeting deadlines once those deadlines have been stated is a make-or-break factor for many new businesses. Setting up always takes longer than planned. Builders always run into problems they had not expected. New technology always clicks into action more patchily than hoped. People get sick. Suppliers or transporters go on strike. But none of that mollifies the customer who expected his consignment to arrive on the fourth of the month. If, on the other hand, you can deliver the stuff to him on the second of the month, he will be a very happy customer. Check first to make sure he is happy to receive it, because if it is something very bulky, he may prefer Just In Time [JIT] deliverybecause it offers him a better period of time in which to clear his warehouse.

The "WHEN?" question is easy to answer in the beginning and more difficult to answer in the longer term. In the beginning, when you only have one client, perhaps, and that client wants 100 of your product, you can promise him that he will have them in two weeks' time. But when you have six clients, and they are beginning to place orders of 300 and 400 at a time, you may be extremely pressured to meet both deadline and demand, especially if you have not anticipated this demand and have based your costings on fewer employees and lower overheads.

In asking the six questions of yourself and your partners, it is most important that you ask the supplementaries, not just the initial questions, and that you disallow any optimistic answers. Numerous businesses have failed because their promoters, in answer to that first apparently simple question "Who's going to buy this product and why?" have said "Lots of people" and "I just *know*." You *don't* just know. Even if people tell you that they have been waiting all their lives for your product, they may be simply encouraging you. Or it may be that in some way your question triggers a self-serving impulse in someone and they would like to think of themselves as the sort of person who *would* buy your product. When push comes to shove, though, they won't. If they say they'd buy your product, try to understand why. Figure out their rationale if you can.

One person on their own is unlikely to get the answers to all six questions. You may have to beg or hire professional advice, whether legal or financial. Or you may have to get more market research done than you can personally get through with your personal questionnaire and clipboard. There are many approaches to market research. Some cost a fortune. Some don't. There are some kinds of surveys which will allow a couple of questions to be tagged on to the end at relatively little cost to the one who tags along. Ask the market research company about this. Or a university department may be able to help you at minimal or no cost by deputing some of its marketing students to complete a study on your behalf.

Whichever way you do your market research, take the end result with a grain of salt and divide every optimistic finding by half. The hills are alive with the sound of weeping from companies which believed their own market research, and not all of the weepers are small, start-up companies, either. The Coca Cola empire was heading for its hundredth birthday when it began to do market research to find out how it could halt the slippage in the sales of its core product: Coke. Not only were people in the Eighties beginning to go for other beverages, ranging from mineral water to fruit juice, but Pepsi, Coke's major competitor, was edging up relentlessly alongside the giant. So Coke began to test a new formula for its popular product, and to do market research on the acceptability of the new taste.

Their tests in the market place of this unnamed new variation on the Coke theme indicated that people loved the taste of it. It was sweeter than coke had traditionally been. So strong were the indications coming from the market research that Coke management decided, in the mid-Eighties, now was the time to make a radical assault on the soft drinks market by doing away with the traditional drink and bringing new Coke to the shops all at once. There were no plans to market the two tastes side by side. It was going to be BC and AC; the Before Coke and the After Coke.

It made a big news story. It also made for a consumer revolt of unprecedented venom, for one simple reason. The market research had homed in on the taste of the new drink, and people certainly approved of that. But the market research had totally ignored the sentimental attachment people had to the old drink, particularly in the US, its home market, and that sentimental attachment began to assert itself within hours of the announcement that traditional coke was to be done away with. Coke hoarding began. Coca Cola headquarters had to instal extra telephone lines to cope with the plethora of shirty phone calls coming in from fans of the traditional drink. Within eleven weeks, the company had wisely climbed down and re-introduced the old drink, re-naming it Coca Cola Classic. They had clearly taken a risk suggested by their corporate direction and supported by market research, the latter, unfortunately, having asked the wrong questions. (It is worth pointing out that the end result of what many called the marketing boob of the century was almost totally good for Coke. When traditional Coca Cola came back, it sold much more than it had been selling previously, presumably because drinkers revived a flagging loyalty to a product they had not realised had significance to much more than their taste buds.)

If you are as big as Coca Cola, you can get away—just about—with asking the wrong questions. If you are a start-up company and you ask the wrong questions, you will be a never-was company very quickly.

There is also the temptation to invest too much significance in numbers. Entrepreneurs are often persuaded into this by having to prepare projections and plans for banks and state sponsored bodies. They agree that a target, justified by their market research, is X hundred units moved per month, growing to Y hundred units by the end of the second year, and those figures attain the certitude of Holy Writ, even though they are plucked out of the air and supported by opinions people do not have to back by putting their money down. According to Daniel Kehrer, Editor of *Independent Business Magazine*, statistics have become a way of purchasing peace of mind for the decision-maker. He writes:

If there's a number, our obsession with statistics says it must have an economic use. A number by itself seems coldly objective. But statistics are easily manipulated or misinterpreted. Statistics do lie. Successful risk-taking companies discover that what *actually* happens and what they *expect* to happen by examining the "evidence" may be radically different things. General Foods found that out when its regional test marketing of a new drink mix product appeared to score a huge success. Sales figures for all flavours of Great

Shakes were high, so company executives gave it a national release. When it flopped, they were puzzled. The numbers had predicted success. General Foods discovered too late that during the test, consumers eager to find a flavour they liked had continued buying them one after another. But they hated them all and stopped buying. This doesn't mean all research or statistics are evil, only that they can be misused by those who disregard chance, change and unpredictability. (*Doing Business Boldly*, 1990)

Before you start your own business and become your own boss, you need a great many statistics about the market and your prospects within that market. You need an awful lot of scepticism about the happier of those statistics, and even greater resilience to get over the depression caused by the scepticism. You need to have deflated and discarded all of your assumptions and replaced them with data-based expectations. And you need to have asked all of the six questions in every conceivable form and said "Oh yeah?" aloud when you have come up against an answer that doesn't have a fact to support it. Only when you have done all this are you ready to craft your business plan.

(And even when you have done all this, there is a strong case for putting, at the end of the business plan, the old slogan that cartographers use to stick at the end of maps where uncharted waters lay: *Hic sunt dracones* or "Here be dragons." A good sound business plan may put your banker's mind at rest, but there still be a lot of dragons out there in the real world where you plan to steer your business.)

With all the answers to hand, you write a business plan which offers the reader:

- A concise and clear statement of your business, including its name, address, age, products or services, targets, financial structure and marketplace position

- A detailed description of the product or service you are offering. By "detailed" we mean that the reader must be acquainted with how you're going to make or supply the commodity or service, how what you have to offer compares with what competitors have to offer, and how you plan to protect any new products you may have developed through patents or copyrights

- An overview of the context into which you are proposing to move, including data on your customers, your competition, conditions in the economy and in the sector of business into which you and your business fit

- A notion of what strategy you plan to follow. This would take in your marketing and sales plans; your method of distribution, if you're selling a product; of delivering the service, if that's where your interests lie; your costings and how much of those costings is absorbed by advertising and promotion

- A picture of how the company is going to be managed and operated. Flow charts, if your company is going to be big enough to merit flow charts. Personnel structure. Expertise of yourself and of the people you plan to employ, if any

- Details on how your company is financed

- Projections which give the reader a grasp of when you plan to be operational, when your break-even date is, etc. This is where you get into nasty charts filled with repetitive figures, most of them having several noughts to them and very little relationship (unless your background is in book-keeping or accountancy) to anything you have done before.

- A summary that says it all very briefly

Keep it as simple as possible and don't spend a fortune getting a consultant to do it.

One wise man we know who has loads of experience in dealing with new companies and their business plans says "Beware of consultants who will offer to prepare a Business Plan that looks terrific. Ribbons. Graphs. Colour pictures. And full of horseshit."

6

Acquiring the Start-Up Money

Let's put the negatives out front here, before we start peeling off the banknotes.

- Never borrow money you don't have to, because compound interest is like insomnia. Worse than you ever thought possible, feels as if it lasts for ever, and is never fully appreciated as a torture except by others in similar *extremis*.

- Never buy anything until there is no alternative.

- Never lease anything you don't have to, because lease agreements are linked directly to your life's blood and only look easy at the beginning.

- Never employ anybody on a permanent basis until their presence will earn the company three times what they cost you.

- Never sell off bits of your small growing company. Sell off bits of your house or family first.

If you live by all of these impossible rules, then you will not need money upfront. But the fact is that you may have to employ someone before you're sure they can earn their keep, you may have to lease equipment, and you may need either bank borrowings or the infusion of capital that selling off a little of your equity will bring. Your business plan will establish precisely how much money you need. It may also provide you with indications as to where you should source that money. But let us add one general millstone around your neck: research into small business failure shows that most fail through lack of working capital. Handing on this weighty observation doesn't really add much to the sum of human knowledge, because it would be just as easy to claim the corollary of the "lack of working capital" statement, which is that the majority of small businesses fail because of poor planning. Or that the majority of small businesses fail because of inadequate management. (Because if you had good managers, they would do the right kind of planning and get the right kind of seed capital, wouldn't they?)

However, the bottom line is that you may need capital and you want to get it on the best terms from the right people.

Essentially, you can get money in three main ways:

1 Grants

2 Loans

3 Venture Capital subscribed by shareholders

Apart from what we describe as the "main" ways, blobs of money can be provided to the new business by savings, by inheritances (you should be so lucky) by a redundancy or early retirement package, by compensation for an accident or by winning the Lottery. About which let us simply pass on the late-acquired wisdom of a friend of ours who got done out of his savings by fraud. "It's no fun to be suddenly without your F— You Money," he says. Meaning that a wee package of savings or compo can literally and metaphorically be the secret finance you need to assure yourself that if things ever go wrong or a boss or colleagues become too much, you can tell them where to shove it. Investing your F— You money in a business is dodgy.

Assuming that you are going to need a bank loan, hear this. You are not just borrowing money. You are starting a relationship with a bank manager. Many people who are their own bosses miss out on this. They get someone else to make the lodgements and to deal with the bank and they do not talk to their bank manager except when the water is hot and rising, whereas they should be seeking to be a known and valued customer whose plans and intentions are understood by the bank manager and the peaks and valleys of whose business are understood in turn by him or her.

In order to get a good relationship going with the person who is going to be your bank manager, it helps to pick the right bank. The fact that you already have a personal account in a given bank may or may not be relevant to the choice. The bank in which you have your personal account may not be interested in providing substantial loans—but then you may not need a substantial loan. A merchant bank like Ansbacher or Guinness and Mahon will not be interested in you, because however ambitious your plans, they don't look with marked enthusiasm at loans below a couple of hundred thousand. Talk to your friends and to your bank manager, if he or she qualifies as a friend, to find out which financial institution you should be starting with, never losing sight of the fact that there are some institutions, such as the ICC, which have a specific development brief, and some, such as the ACC, which are eager to be active in more than their core (in this case, farming) business. Do *not* go to your bank to cash a cheque for fifty quid, and, on impulse while you're there, decide to lay your plans in a wild splurge of half-worked-out detail on your bank manager's unprepared mind. When you want to talk business, get your Business Plan typed up, get a friend to read through it with the promise of a tenner for every typo or wrong figure they spot, get the flaws fixed, and send it to the Bank Manager in advance of the meeting you will then civilly seek to have with said Bank Manager. Perhaps a week in advance; you want him to have an understanding of the type and thrust of your business before the two of you get down to discussing financial details. There are three kinds of borrowings. You may need one of them, or a combination of more than one. They are short term, medium term and long term.

- Long-Term Borrowings

Usually for the purpose of acquiring long term assets. The payments on the money borrowed relate to the life expectancy of the asset acquired. A mortgage to buy a house or a factory building is a long-term borrowing. You may take fifteen or twenty years to pay it back.

- Medium-Term Borrowings

This would be where you might take out a loan of, say, £25,000 over a period of three to five years, typically to buy plant, machinery, office equipment or computers.

- Short-Term Borrowings

Here, the typical example is an overdraft. An overdraft does not mean that you borrow money immediately. It means that there is a specified leeway within your bank account which allows you to go into an agreed level of debt at particular times. This helps you cope with the gap between you delivering your goods or services and actually getting paid for them. It also helps you cope with seasonality, if your business is affected by passing time. So if you produce an item which is aimed at the pre-Christmas market, you will need money to produce it in the summer and to tide you over until January, when the shops begin to pay *you* the money customers paid *them* for your product.

You are unlikely to be able to work out how much borrowing you need in a form acceptable to your Bank Manager without going through the business plan process. But before you ever cast your financial needs into a shape to please the financiers, you need to do the sums and establish your borrowing needs to your own satisfaction. It is a critical decision because if you get it wrong, you can either end up scratching around and not being able to develop your business properly if you borrow too little or, if you borrow too much, end up with huge repayments that you can't afford, resulting from unnecessary spending done because the money was there. So again, if you're serious about the business that you're going into, you have to sit down and try to estimate your real financial needs. It's a matter of fair-minded guesswork, although you don't need to let your bank manager know that.

You hold conversations with yourself: "Look, if I get the jobs that I think I'll get, how much income will I have and what are my expenses going to be?"

Develop a worst scenario. Develop a best scenario. Settle on somewhere in between and then continue your internal conversation about the pattern of your business and the implications of that pattern. "I think I'll take in, say, £50,000 in my first year in business. I think it's going to come in in this kind of way. This is what I'm going to need in terms of equipment - equipment to get me started."

Putting all of those down on paper together will give you a very good fix on the kind of money that you need. Don't underborrow or don't undercapitalise your business but if the bank say, "We'll give you £50,000" and you think you'll only need £30,000, take your thirty and keep the other twenty in reserve. You might call down on it at a future stage when you continue to grow, but don't take too much initially. One of the very few advantages of a personal guarantee is that it tends to stimulate realism and moderation in the novice borrower. If you know that your personal guarantee of £50,000 means that £50,000 worth of your personal property is suddenly endangered, you begin to manage just fine on a borrowed £25,000.

Track record is very important when it comes to getting money from a bank. So if you have a well-managed personal account with a particular branch then your own bank manager is the person to approach first.

If you're looking for five hundred quid to expand a little hobby making chicken pies for the local corner shop baking midnight and week-ends while holding down the day job in the civil service—no problem. You'll get your £500 without any difficulty because the bank is not depending on your sale of chicken pies to get their money back.

If, however, you decide to look for £50,000 to start selling your chicken pies to Japan that's a different story. The bank will want to know you've researched your project well. Who wants to buy your product? Who are your competitors? Why will people buy your product rather than your competitor's? Costings for your raw materials, machinery, premises, transport will need to be incorporated into financial projections for maybe three years ahead in the form of cashflow statements, forecast profit and loss accounts and balance sheets.

Banks like a business plan that has been professionally prepared. If your experience lies in the making of chicken pies and you don't have a clue about finance, then the bank will like you a lot if you use a well known accountant. (But shop around— listen to our adviser on page 158.)

They also like it when you have experience and expertise in the business field you're going into.

You, the person, will need to be exposed also along with your business plan. This does seem like big brother coming to live in your ear but if you have three kids at school, a mortgage, a father-in-law in the spare room, two dogs and a canary sapping up your annual earnings of £X and your projected earnings in the new business is £X minus £5,000, then it won't be such a "viable proposition" (bank-speak) to your bank manager, or to you for that matter. Your personality is also important. Bank managers love solid citizens who can talk figures, who look healthy, yet are driven to succeed, who are calm yet energetic. Sort of like Noddy crossed with Big Ears and just a touch of Desperate Dan.

How you actually get the money from the bank will depend on what you need it for. If you need £50,000 the bank may decide to give you a package which will be tailored to meet your needs such as money for raw materials, a building, machinery in the form of an overdraft or maybe leasing.

What about personal guarantees?

"In the limited company situation we look for a personal guarantee and we may even look for them supported in the form of a life policy or shares—

some tangible security," one bank manager told us. "A limited company is a legal entity and nobody is the company. Somebody has to be answerable to the bank. If there are no directors tied into a limited company in a wind-up situation—that's it. It's gone. Usually we look for tangible support and security."

"Like a house?" we asked.

"A family home is not attractive to us. We're not interested in second mortgages on the family home because our bank is not in the business of putting people out on the side of the street. We'd be looking for the holiday home in the west. Everyone goes into business to make vast amounts of money. Why should the bank give unsecured money? If you have any doubts about signing a letter of guarantee then you've doubts about your business. If you're 100% certain you've no doubts or worries about signing." (Who the hell can be 100% certain about *anything*, we ask?)

If at all possible avoid personal guarantees. Banks are not gamblers. They are places where you can rent money. One wag commented that they will lend you money as long as you can prove you don't need it. Because they're not in the risk business, they try their best to get you to guarantee your own money. In the nicest possible way. A bank person will say, "If you have the amount of faith in your business that you say you have, then you've no problem with a personal guarantee and all that's left is to sign this bit of paper." That's all that hits you at that particular time. You would feel grudging if you refused. You would feel you were in some way cheating the bank.

I mean, just a signature on that wee bit of paper? If, however, your business unfortunately goes bad on you and the company cannot afford to make the repayment to the bank, goes into liquidation or stops trading, then the bank can come after you for the balance. People have had to go out and borrow the money from another bank or building society to meet repayments on a loan, because the bank called in personal guarantees. The bank's personal guarantees are watertight from a legal point of view. So if the business goes wallop (God between us and all harm) you may be caught on the sharp edge of a personal guarantee. Even in this worst of scenarios, a good relationship with your bank manager might just mean that you may not have to pay the full amount. Negotiate on it. If at all possible, do not even start down the personal guarantee road. You are an entrepreneur, not a mendicant, as *Commencements* owner Jane Williams proved when she was starting out.

"I went to the bank when I wanted to invest in some computer equipment and said 'I want to do this short term, I want an overdraft for it. A smallish overdraft—and you're not getting a personal guarantee!' And they said 'We don't do it without a personal guarantee,' and I said, 'Well then, I'll go elsewhere.' They came up with the money and I've had nothing but a really good relationship with them. So much so that now, they're shoving a quarter of a million at me to buy a building and I've said now is not the time to buy a building."

Leasing may also be an option in the short term. A lease is when you go in to buy a piece of equipment and a leasing company charges you on a monthly basis for the particular piece of equipment. At the end of the lease they will transfer it either to you or to a third party at a figure that depends on the amount that you've paid during the period.

When considering leasing something, shopping around is a must. First of all, you need to shop at the right time. Towards the end of the leasing company's tax year, for example, you can get a much more favourable rate than at other times because Ireland's tax laws mean that the leasing company can get a quick tax write-off at some stages.

Not only will different leasing companies charge you different rates throughout the run of the lease, but different leasing companies have a different price they charge you to buy at the end of the period. The leasing company effectively own the asset and allow you use it, but at the end of the leasing period you have to buy the asset from them. In our experience one particular bank charged virtually double what another bank charged the investor in leasing. So you've got that factor to watch as well. Check out not only the monthly repayments but also the buy-out at the end of the period.

There are two different types of leases applying to cars and similar necessities. If you, for example, buy a car that's costing £10,000 you can have what's called a finance lease which means that you're paying the full cost of the car over a three-year period and at the end of that you've little or nothing to pay to own the car. The other is called an operating lease which means you pay a lower charge over the three years but only pay the depreciation costs of the car. Thus, to own the car at the end of the leasing period you have to pay a lump sum.

It's important to know the difference between these two types of leases because if you don't, when you're trying to negotiate one, you may not be aware of the buying cost at the end of it; one lease might seem an awful lot more attractive but at the end of the leasing period you have no asset. You have to do some personal tailoring here. Which is more important to your business—to have a car with a low lease rent cost and in three years time cope with the cost of replacing the car, or to say "I'm going to have that extra bit of cash because of the nature of the business"? Don't feel the need to buy/lease a new car or van—bankers, backers, customers even, are far happier to see you start off with a banger rather than start with a BMW and end up with a bang.

This is the sort of problem/opportunity any start-up business faces, which is never properly left to financial advisers, because financial advisers know the business of *business*. They don't know *your* business, which reflects your skills, traits, attitudes, strengths, weaknesses and—yes—whims.

Another determinant worth mentioning in relation to leasing is the tax angle. When you're buying from a leasing company, they will charge you VAT on most rentals. If you're registered for VAT that really doesn't have a huge impact on you. If it's computers, or plant machinery, you can reclaim the VAT. Unfortunately this doesn't apply to cars because the VAT legislation doesn't allow it. If however, you're in what's called an exempt business for VAT such as crèches, colleges or schools and you don't have to register for VAT, leasing can be more expensive because you have 23% VAT on your lease rent. If you fund the same asset through a term loan in the bank, your repayments will be fairly similar but you won't have the 23% VAT to pay.

When an accountancy partnership or business consultancy is putting together the financial package for a new business, they often create a mix—so much borrowings, so much grant aid, so much investment, so much leasing. If you know that the company needs say £30,000 to get up and running and you're prepared to put £10,000 in yourself, the bank might lend you £10,000 and the IDA grant-aid you to the tune of £10,000. This is a normal kind of mix. You may put £10,000 into shares or you may put £2 into shares and make a loan to the company of the other £9,998. However one of the advantages of putting money in the form of shares is that it would reduce any capital gains payable if you dispose of your shares.

Sometimes if the IDA are putting in £10,000 they want your loan subordinated to theirs. In other words, you can't repay yourself so long as the IDA grants are outstanding.

• Venture Capital

About venture capital we prefer to say relatively little. In a start-up situation, your most likely investors are you, you and you. Plus your brother, your mother and your best pal, if they have any money. Yes, there are venture capital companies around—a great many more than there used to be. They are sometimes interested in a green field situation, but not very often. Where a green field or start-up business attracts them, it is either because the people involved pack a hell of a collective punch, or because the business looks like being a "definition" business. (OK, there are lots of companies out there making computer floppy discs, but this company is going to change that whole business and be the Sony, the Rolls Royce, the Hoover, the Dr Scholl of the floppies.)

A number of the venture capital companies would put money into companies on the understanding that they would make a capital gain at the end of the period, very often by getting those companies to go on the stock market, or—less often—by selling the shares back to the promoters at the end of a five-year or ten-year period (usually a five-year period).

If you're starting up your own business, the need to give serious attention to venture capital is years down the road.

Much the same applies to the Business Expansion Scheme. The BES has been like a hit record that started life as a "sleeper." The BES existed without causing many waves for several years, and then, around about 1988, a great many people sat up and took notice of it as a way of tax-effectively investing in growing companies. In that year, more money was raised under the scheme by companies than had been raised in all of the previous four years. BES means that an individual can invest between

IR£200 and £25,000 per year in a qualifying company and obtain tax relief at the highest rate. It is—rightly—hedged around with all sorts of rules and regulations. To be a "qualifying company," for instance, the firm has to be a manufacturer, must provide a service which receives employment grants under the IDA's International Services Programme, must be in shipping or Special Trading House activities (don't ask, you probably don't qualify under this one) or fit into the category of "tourist undertaking." That's by no means all. In addition the company getting the money must be incorporated in the Republic of Ireland and be liable for Irish tax, but cannot be quoted on the Stock Exchange or USM, although it can be quoted on the Smaller Companies Market.

Because BES means a significant loss of revenue to the Exchequer, its very success constantly provokes legislators to observe it closely and to nip it and tuck it if it looks like becoming too successful. One entrepreneur we talked to, who might very well qualify for BES, chose not to, because three weeks of initial and exploratory meetings with accountants was logging up billable hours on their part (billable to *him*) and creating for him the idea that he had to structure, shape and interpret his company with enormous sophistry in order to qualify.

"I was trying to explain to my wife one night what I had been listening to all day and now half-understood, and she suddenly went glazed on me," he says. "I thought I had lost her, and I started to go back over what I was saying, but she said no, she understood it fine, she was just bored with it. I was

173

totally flummoxed. We were in this together and even though there had been difficult and tiring things before, she'd never reacted so dismissively. So I sat there in silence and she tore up all the notes she had made and told me it seemed to her like a very simple choice. I could either be an entrepreneur or I could be a Jesuit! At this stage I was worse than flummoxed. 'You have an idea for a business that'll work,' she told me. 'It'll work because you're very good at your craft, you're very good at delegating and motivating other people. If you spend any more time playing around with definitions and qualifications and ifs and buts and maybes, sure, you may get BES investment, but it'll be investment in nothing, going nowhere, because you'll have taken yourself away from what you're good at and tackled something which requires a combination of all of the skills and talents you don't have.' " He shrugs. "When I got over the blow, the truth of it was inescapable. So I abandoned it and we set up without it. And it was a success. Maybe not as tax-effective a success as it would have been under the BES, but a lot more time- and satisfaction-effective."

Whether it's venture capital, a loan from your bank or a good leasing deal, you need to shop around, have a clear and conservative but not cripplingly conservative estimate of what you want and why you want it, and you need, above all, never to lose sight of the business you are in. The business you are in is craftwork, or telling executives how to power dress, or making doughnuts at dawn. It isn't running between banks and being flattered by the transient respectful attention of bank managers and advisers, at least some of whose respectful attention is being paid for on an hourly basis, by you.

Preventing disaster when you seek finance is best done by avoiding totally predictable pitfalls. An excellent free booklet called *Running Your Own Business*, produced by the IDA and Stokes Kennedy Crowley and available from either body free of charge, summarises the most frequent reasons behind the failure of new companies to get loans or investment capital:

- Weaknesses in management (such as lack of motivation, financial acumen, marketing ability or an impressive track record)

- Inadequate personal finance (which can often indicate lack of commitment)

- Poorly presented proposals

- Inadequate security offered

- Too many risks inherent in the venture

- Over-ambitiousness

- Lack of detail as to how the finance will be repaid

- Product or service weaknesses

- Markets not properly researched

7

Getting Paid, Making a Profit

So there was this brand new company which was set up to manufacture a new product. The company owners did their market research and established that there was clearly a gap to be filled by what they were producing. They produced it to the highest quality possible. They marketed it thoughtfully and persistently. It sold. They had it priced correctly. They went broke. *Because people didn't pay them for it.*

Couldn't happen? Uh, uh. It has happened. Repeatedly. It does happen—is happening even as we speak. It will happen in the future. Repeatedly.

It happens for two reasons:

1. The company doing the buying has, as part of its policy, a determination to delay paying for as long as possible.

2. The company doing the selling places a low priority on asking for money.

Reason one arises, not from contempt for the seller, but from a very decided interpretation of the role of money, perhaps best expressed to us by an industrialist we talked to, who rated credit control and money management as his salient skills as a boss.

"I employ eighteen people here," this man told us. "Eighteen people—and Money. Money is not a separate issue, it is an employee. Now if Money is *here* on my staff, available to me, then I can make a profit out of it. If I have to let Money go off to work for someone else, I'm at a loss for that employee. So I get Money in as quickly as possible from other people, and I hold Money as long as I possibly can— as long as my creditors will let me."

Creditors of this man will tell you, sourly, that he doesn't pay in thirty days or sixty days or ninety days. He doesn't pay at all until he gets a solicitor's letter. This he will not confirm, but he gives the reasoning behind his tight-fistedness. It is reasoning that suits the side of the fence he is on, and does nothing much for the people on the creditor's side of the same fence.

"Let's say you can get 10% interest on a deposit in the bank," he says. "Now, next Tuesday, I get a delivery of goods worth one hundred pounds. I can pay the hundred pounds straight away or very quickly, and the supplier will think I'm a real decent skin. Great. Fantastic. Can you imagine me telling my bank manager that a supplier thinks I'm a decent skin for quick paying? My supplier is a nice guy, but I can't afford to care that he thinks I'm a decent skin, because remember, I have this employee called Money, and I have £100 of it, and if I shove it in the bank for a year, I will then own £110 because of the interest rate. So I can either keep my money and make it work for me, or pay it out to someone else. I pay late. What else would I do?"

Some companies simply pay as slowly as they possibly can, and are known to take that approach. A small company can be extremely vulnerable in such circumstances, and its vulnerability will be magnified by an unplumbed postulate that the purchasing company will come through with the readies quickly. Not only do companies *not* come through with the readies quickly under normal circumstances, but many of them will hide behind any handy hedge to excuse even later payment. Whenever there has been a bank strike, part of the tidying up afterwards is the garbage-bagging of companies pulled down by debtors who used the bank strike as an excuse for extending their credit further than the supplying company could handle. Another factor which tends to bring out the worst in people is a rumour going around that Company Hopeful is doing badly. People who owe Company Hopeful money may raise their shoulders up round their ears and slow down their payments, knowing that Company Hopeful is going to be tied up trying to pay off the people to whom *they* owe money and who, rendered frantic by the rumours, are demanding instant payment before Company Hopeful goes into liquidation. One of the great sad truths of business is that people who are caring, decent, honourable, public-spirited and committed to the preservation of the ozone layer will, once you slap a corporate identity over them, do things that are uncaring, indecent, dishonourable, inhumane and generally pretty disgusting. Witness the Dalkon Shield, the contraceptive device which killed and maimed women and their babies, and which was marketed long after the evidence had arrived proving it faulty. It was marketed by a company of (up to then) the highest reputation in the health-care business. Witness the motor companies which, if Ralph Nadar had not so relentlessly exposed them to public scrutiny, would have continued to leave cars on the road which had been proven to explode and burn, killing their drivers, in certain types of collisions.

Sometimes, of course, the company owing you money is in trouble itself, and that's where the small company (yours) which is awaiting a long overdue payment may be of relatively little importance to the troubled larger company. A large company can be closed because it owes VAT or PAYE or because a bank forecloses. Large companies which are going through a period of near-insolvency are rarely closed down by a small company to which they owe money. We came across an example of where this had worked to the benefit of the larger company and to the consequent detriment not just of the smaller company, but of those to whom the smaller company owed money. It went like this: Kiddywinks Ltd., (not its real name) was the small company. A happy partnership of bright entrepreneurs with a great idea and endless energy. They "sold" their project to a large company as a venture the large company would incorporate into its national publicity. Then the large company experienced a downturn in its market but contracts had been signed, and the twenty-year-olds running Kiddywinks were undisturbed when the first half of their payment failed to come through on the day promised. They had the respect of the small for the large, and the confidence of children that parents will never die. Also, they were very busy. They were commissioning work to be done, articles of furniture to be made, premises to be leased, and they went right on doing that, because they were honest and innocent. Meanwhile the large company, protected from undue scrutiny by a fast-talking PR company which knew which side its bread was buttered on (because its bread had been buttered in advance of the work being done) was scrabbling around trying to arrange an un-threatening merger before the full facts hit the fan. The large company failed. The PR company got all grave and solemn and produced a press release that would make your eyes well up with unshed tears. Large company is in receivership, it said. Large company, it went on, started by Boe Joggs back in 1934. Boe Joggs, honoured by his home town as Proud Son Of in 1956. Company has specialised in a high quality, premium brand dingdong which has achieved a world reputation, but ran into problems outside of its control when X happened. Quote from Boe Joggs Jr, saying that this is a sad day for him and his family and he makes no bones about including all his employees under the heading "Family..."

Eventually, some of the companies which were owed money by Boe Joggs got paid about twenty pence for every quid that was due to them. The ones who got paid didn't include Kiddywinks Ltd., because they couldn't wait. Once the word hit the streets that their biggest, indeed *only* customer was kaput, all of the people to whom Kiddywinks owed money came and camped on their door, and because they were honest and terrified, they signed cheques until the cheque-book died. First come, first served. Not all of the people who got cheques benefitted from them, because there were rather more pages in the chequebook than there were pound notes in their account. One other small company, started only five years before Kiddywinks, found, the next day, when they delivered the major order they had received from this new business, that the headquarters was locked up and the phone was dead. This other small company could not sell the order to anybody else, because it had the Kiddywinks' logo all over it, and they got no money whatever out of the deal.

"That was 1985," the MD recalls. "That was our fifth year of business. That was the year we were going to break into modest profit. Instead, we had a bad debt of twenty thousand pounds on our books and no profit at all. It was an incredible thump in the mouth. But you learn even from thumps in the mouth. We learned two lessons from that. One was to control credit much more tightly. To get paid deposits on some orders, half up front on others. The second was to be much more ruthless when people were slow payers. Now, once a month, I go out to maybe three companies that owe us money, and I go to the receptionist and explain that I've come for an overdue payment. Sometimes that in itself is enough. Someone rings the Accounts department and probably says 'Jesus, we have this man standing right here in front of us saying you haven't paid and they were due to get it fourteen days ago, send someone down here with a cheque.' As I say, sometimes it works, and some poor sod from a low level in that department is sent down with a cheque and an excuse that'd embarrass a two-year old. Sometimes it doesn't work, and what happens then is that I smile warmly at the receptionist who has just told me dismissively that nobody can deal with me now, and I say 'OK. Tell you what. I'm going to sit down here and read *Business & Finance* magazine from your coffee table and wait until someone CAN come and pay me.' She then gets flustered and says well someone mightn't be able to see me for hours, and I get even happier.'No problem,' I say, beaming like a little smile badge. 'If I finish *Business & Finance*, I can read *Management*, because I see you have it, too. I have all the time in the world. I'll wait until closing time, if need be, and stay after you've all gone home! Ho, ho ho.' Then, awash in my own merriment, I go over and sit down and start to read *Business & Finance*, because I believe I probably *should* read it anyway, but rarely get the time to do it in the office, and usually before I'm past the centrefold my problem has been solved. Only once ever did a company push it so that they were trying to get me out of the premises at closing time and beginning to look like they would lay hands on me. Which would have been a *big* mistake. Normally, I stay very pleasant, I get the results I'm looking for, and that purchaser doesn't usually try to string us out again."

Jane Williams, founder of the *Commencements* company, believes that getting money out of customers in Ireland is more difficult than in certain other countries.

"People in Ireland don't pay," she observes. "They'll string you out for sixty or ninety days if they can. These are people you know and you've done really good work for them but they'll still do that because it's the system. It's not the system elsewhere, you get paid elsewhere. But getting paid takes a lot of effort and it can be difficult in the kind of close relationship we typically build with our clients. If it were an objective relationship, it's easier to say 'hang on a minute here, you've got that, I'm taking it back unless you pay me for it.' In the consulting side of things, it's not that easy. You do need that belief in yourself to be able to say 'I've done a good job for you and you should pay me and our contract is that you pay me.'"

Reminders and nags should be done in what ever way is most effective. We were told of one small company where the bookkeeper does a highly theatrical moral blackmail based on the premise that she personally is going to lose her job if she cannot produce this overdue cheque for her bullying boss. (Her "bullying" boss, a man of vague gentleness who regards killing flies as genocide, was startled to hear himself described in these terms when he came into his bookkeeper's office behind her one day and heard her in mid-performance on the telephone.) Other companies find that varying the level of the phonecaller works. The first reminder call is by a secretary in the accounts department. The second is from a department manager. The third is from the assistant to the MD. Now this is a small, non-hierarchical company but they give themselves roles in order to impress non-payers. Still other companies rely on humour, sending repeat statements with little plaintive stickers on them, operating on the theory that if there is a human being in the Accounts Department, he or she may be tickled enough by the sticker to consider paying the overdue bill. A US cartoonist has taken this a step further, by creating a book of pull-out FAX cover sheets, which attract the attention of the company to which they are sent by virtue of their unusual design, and which mitigate the bluntness of their message with a touch of humour. (Not only does this seem like a bright idea for extracting money from those who owe it, but it also seems to us a great product idea for a new small business. Very little creativity has gone into FAX documentation design, and FAXes are taking over the world, so there has to be a market there.)

The problems small businesses have with slow payers are not unique to Ireland. On average, British firms wait for 78 days before they're paid on foot of an invoice which stated that it must be paid within thirty days, and, as a result, it is estimated that British small firms, at any given time, are owed in the region of £100 billion. A study by an English credit control company, *Intrum Justitia*, revealed that in 1990, letting customers have an extra forty-eight days of credit was equivalent to 5.7% of the average business's turnover, and often added up to half its potential profit. What the study showed was that many small companies that borrowed money for quite another purpose often ended up using it to fill the gap arising because of unpaid bills.

The standard credit period varies between countries, too. In Ireland, most bills expect to be paid within thirty days, and say so. (Reality may be a sad let-down, but those are the standard credit terms for many products and services.) In Italy, the same bill might quote a sixty-day term. If you are not aware of that when you export to that country, you can age quite a bit as you await payment.

Another downside to the matter of late payment by overseas customers is called currency fluctuations. Currency fluctuations can mean that a product which you could have exported last week by the crate-load you can't export this week at all, because it would cost too much to the customers in the country you wanted to export to. So you either ship the crates at a loss to your company, to ensure that your market share is retained, or you hold on to the crates in the hope that the currency will fluctuate back to where it suits you, that you can get the order at that time, and that the goods will not rot in the interim. Currency fluctuations can do enormous and very public damage to a company like Waterford Glass, which exports so much of its product, and they can do enormous and very private damage to a small start-up company which has just broken into the export market. This was what happened to *Chesneau*, a company producing elegant leather briefcases, handbags and purses in Kilkenny.

"I work with my husband. We came to Ireland about fifteen years ago to learn English—I'm from Spain, Edmund is from France," says Carmen Chesneau. "My family background is self-employed; my father is a watch-maker, my mother a painter. When I was doing ceramics and drawing in the Art College, I first started to make little purses just to pay the rent. Then came the decision for the two of us—were we going to leave this country or stay here? We stayed and began a business about ten years ago and, looking back, I know we didn't get good advice, and we started just as craftworkers, not as businesspeople. But we began to produce good quality work and won a number of awards, and we attracted attention in Kilkenny and began to export. It all seemed great—and then we got caught in the export market by currency fluctuations, and I don't think we were alone; there were other people in the fashion business caught as well, because I think there was too much pressure to export without having first of all built up a good strong home base. But we were doing very well in the United States market, had contracts with really prestigious people like Ralph Lauren, and then suddenly the dollar went bang and we were locked in for the season with our pricing. We were stuck with these prices for six months and they were killing us, and we could see disaster coming up and there was just nothing we could do about it, and the company folded. But we are fighters by nature and we just decided we have a really beautiful high quality product and lots of other great businesses have gone bang before and started up again. Ralph Lauren, for example, went out of business twice before he really made it. So we started up all over again, but this time we did it in a better way. The IDA and CTT and the Crafts Council all welcomed us back. The IDA, for example, made us the winners of their best product award the first year we were back in action, which was like saying 'We're behind you.' The banks, now, that was a different matter. We're only beginning to get out of their bad books now. My attitude is different now, too. I won't give personal guarantees. In order to get capital, we took in a partner, and he sees our skills, we see his skills; it works very well. We are back up to employing about the same number of people as we were employing when the American dollar took us out, but the last time, it was like a big mushroom growing up, whereas now, it is solid. Very solid."

There is a foreign currency cover which is what the banks call a forward contract to cover against drastic fluctuations in exchange rates. If, for example, you sign a six-month contract with a buyer in the USA for $5,000, you can, if the punt/dollar exchange rate is good on a particular day, agree a rate with your bank (which includes their mark-up.) When you get paid by the US client you must use that rate with your bank. You can do the same if you are buying raw materials in dollars.

Because currency fluctuations can have such an impact on corporate finances, many multi-nationals have incorporated into their financial systems a sophisticated means of maximising benefit from those fluctuations. One Irish consultancy which was doing a good deal of work overseas was puzzled by the fact that some of the bills going to a big continental customer got paid within days, and some of them took months to clear. The small Irish operation eventually asked their contact in the Accounts Department of the continental company.

"We pay you when our computer tells us to pay you," the purchaser said, as if this was so obvious it was scarcely worth saying.

"But why does your computer tell you sometimes

to pay fast and sometimes to pay so slowly, a baby could get born quicker?" he was asked.

"The computer receives the international currency levels every day," the customer said. "And its software triggers payment to you when the currency ratios favour us most. If the currency goes our way next week, you'll get paid next week. If the currency favours *you* for the next month, you won't get paid."

When you are your own boss, then one of your priorities must be getting the best mileage you can for your money. That means knowing what you're owed, when it is due, and having a method of pursuit. You can get as friendly as you like with your customers, but they are still your customers, and you won't live if you don't get paid. (One man who is his own boss is a surgeon, and although you might not think surgeons would have problems pulling in their large fees, one surgeon told us that after ten years in the profession, he learned a bitter financial lesson; patients who get to know you well enough to call you by your first name don't pay you.)

It may be worth your while to stimulate a positive response on the part of people who owe you money by offering them a discount if they settle within a specified time.

If you have neither the time nor the skill to go and winkle the money out of people personally, you may like to consider factoring. Factoring is a deal you do with a financial institution that basically buys your debts. You go along to a factor house and they will say "Give us the right to collect all your debts, and we'll give you, say, eighty per cent of what they're worth up front." The factors have the hassle and the risk, and you have then the use of eighty per cent of the money immediately. It is assured but quite expensive cash flow, and many small companies prefer to persuade and cajole money out of customers they value rather than hand the task over to a third party, no matter how efficient that third party might be.

Getting maximum mileage out of your money is not just a matter of getting that money in quickly. It's also a matter of not tying up that money in stock. The Japanese helped to teach us that if you have to have huge warehouses filled with goods, you have probably spent money you could use for other purposes to pay for the goods you're storing. They invented Just In Time delivery; where you don't take or pay for things you need until you actually need them. Not next month. Not next week. Right now.

Another element in getting mileage out of your money is doing deals. Begging for special treatment or going to the people who will give you special treatment. Just as some banks are particularly welcoming to new start-up companies because at least some of tomorrow's giants are starting small and doing it now, so some business establishments, particularly consultancies, are willing to be a little more than businesslike with a new company. They may even be helpful. Carr Communications, for example, has a long-standing policy of offering its services in training and public relations at half price to companies in their first year of operation.

"We remember our own tough early years," Chairman Bunny Carr says, "And we know we've continued to do business with people who were helpful to us at that time. So we've continued the practice. It's not totally altruistic. First of all, there is the chance that the company will go places and we will continue to provide our services to them—but at normal price as the years go on. Secondly, it puts us working with companies at their most exciting and challenging and least cynical stage, which is always great fun."

According to Pam Kearney, a partner with Dublin accountants O'Hare Barry, overtrading is one of the most fundamental errors you can make in a business when you have got it off the ground and it is expanding. Overtrading can lead very quickly to bankruptcy or liquidation if uncorrected, but often goes uncorrected because the business is expanding and turnover rising, so everybody's happy, while in fact, it is those very factors which are endangering the enterprise. Pam Kearney identifies three ways of avoiding overtrading:

1. Do not increase sales figures at all costs. A high turnover does not necessarily mean you are making good profits. For example, if a business employs five staff for sales of £100,000 and the profit is £10,000, what will the profit be on sales of £200,000? £20,000? NO!

Profit does not increase in direct proportion to sales. To achieve the additional £100,000 turnover you may need to buy new premises, buy new machinery, take on additional staff and so on, so that you could end up making the same level of profits on twice the turnover if you are not careful. (Who was it who said "turnover is vanity, profits are sanity"?)

2. How do you know if you are overtrading? You have a cash crisis generally caused because your margins are too low. You keep your margins tight because the competition is severe and you do not want to lose customers. However, if you have cut your margins too much to increase your sales you might find yourself running into losses and eventually this will lead to a cash crisis.

3. The only way to make sure that you do not fall into the overtrading trap is by producing a sound business plan. You need to take a good long hard look at your business, decide on your most profitable areas and concentrate on those.

The last of those factors is arguably the most difficult for the person who has started a new business and is operating as their own boss, because they have so little chance to stand back and analyse their business, so they get into the position of the apocryphal woodcutter. This particular apocryphal woodcutter being the one who was meeting a pre-winter demand for logs and chopping down and decimating tree after tree. (We're not talking rain forest here. These were fast-growing renewable resource-type trees.) He's turning out the same number of logs each day, but he's getting up earlier and going to work at dawn and coming home after dusk. Eventually a pal happens to see him at work and realises that his axe has been so blunted by all the hard work that it is now not cutting half so efficiently as it should.

"Why don't you sharpen the axe?" asks the pal.

The apocryphal woodcutter fixes him with a look of blind hate, as all of us do when somebody with less work than we have comes up with a bright suggestion.

"Can't you see I'm too busy?" he demands. "I have all these logs to cut..."

Many a person who is their own boss fails to find the time to work out what earns them money and what doesn't. There are some activities done by a company which have nothing to do with making money and if they're not constantly watched, you will have people making reports on the reports of other people following the meeting held to clarify an earlier report about the suggestion that we have handles, rather than ring pulls, on our gizmo. There are clients who spend a lot of money with us and who should be nurtured, and clients who spend much less money with us. It is a cliché of business that twenty per cent of your clients provide eighty per cent of your earnings, and eighty per cent of your clients take up almost all of your time. Finally, there are the products you make or the services you provide that you enjoy making or providing, but when closely examined are found to be grossly time-intensive, and not only that but to demand the time of the most harassed person. As your own boss, you have to learn that what makes you feel warm, unique and fulfilled is not necessarily the thing which will make your business feel warm and profitable. If there is a conflict, find a way to express yourself and earn your self-esteem outside of the business, but do not waste your money and the money of other people by devoting time and passion to a product which will never sell at a price which would justify that time and passion. When you are your own boss, you are in the business of *business*, not in the business of self-regard, and because you *are* your own boss, it often has to be you who brings such cold realism constantly to the attention of the Top Banana: *you*.

8

One Hundred Streetwise Marketing Tips

Not all bosses see marketing as central to their job. Not all people thinking about setting up their own businesses think of it as central.

But it is. Because you could have the most marvellous product in the world, produced by a staff of unrivalled skill, cleanliness and charm in a plant where every aspect of the administration is punctilious and punctual, and you could still see the entire thing hit the skids if you don't do your marketing right.

One dictionary definition of "marketing" at first glance looks unhelpful. "Attendance upon a market," it says. Curtly. And accurately. Because dancing attendance upon your market, or creating the context in which you can sell something, is what ensures that the bottom line of your business, at the end of the year, is in black rather than red. Attending to a market is a complexity of obligations, including learning from the marketplace, shaping your product to meet its needs, packaging it to attract market attention, publicising it so that people are aware of it before they see it on the shelf and getting it delivered on time to the right place at the right price. Nor is it a once-off activity. Attendance upon a market has to be a continuing valued function of your company.

It starts with research. Now, hold *on*. Do not reach for the Golden Pages to find the names of six market research companies. Research takes a lot of forms, not all of them require the involvement of market research companies, and even where they do, a better result is achieved when the client company has a clearly defined objective for the research. Knows what questions it wants asked, in other words, and why.

You start, therefore, by making lists of things you would like to know. Never mind how you will get the answers, at this stage. Just list the questions. We asked one start-up would-be Boss to make a list of what he would like to know about the potential market for his new business, which was a machine, somewhere between an air conditioner and a humidifier, which he had patented and planned to sell to people as an enhancement for their homes. After a week this is what we got back:

Things I would Like to Know

- Has anything like this been on the market here before?

- Will price be a major factor? (I could sell it to a few people at £300 or to a lot of people at £170.)

- Is packaging going to matter?

- Is support from someone like the medical profession going to matter?

- Should I sell it through big hardware shops or mail order (because installation isn't complicated) or put trucks on the road with technicians?

- Do I need a logo and brand name?

- Do I need advertising?

- What makes people buy machines like this?

- Does it matter that it's all made in Ireland?

- Do I need to have a telephone service where people's questions can be answered?

- Do I need to have PR, and what is PR anyway?

- If I had PR would I have to be in it because I don't want to be on TV?

- Can my premises be in an industrial estate, or is that "down market"?

- Would I need a salesman out on the road knocking on doors?

- Can you pay a salesman totally out of what he earns or do you have to pay a salary and then a commission?

- How much of a back-up service would I have to have?

- If people buy this and like it, should I have some system for going back to them and selling them the natural insect repellent thing I'm planning to develop for barbecues?

- Do I need to appear at exhibitions with the product, and do I go to Better Homes exhibitions or medical exhibitions or what?

- If I were selling it door to door, are there particular neighbourhoods where I should concentrate?

- If I was concentrating in one particular neighbourhood, how would I get them to know about the product in advance of sending in sales reps?

- Would I need the sales reps in cars that had the logo all over them?

- Would the installers need to be in an identified uniform?

- Should I start in a shop with one employee and sell over the counter and show people how to install the yoke themselves?

As you can see, some of the questions could be followed up by the man himself. A bit of to-ing and fro-ing among hardware and homecare shops would establish in an informal, but nonetheless accurate way whether or not there was already anything on the market which was in the same line as his gadget. More formal market research (possibly by means of focus group discussions which establish attitudes, rather than door-to-door questioning on shopping patterns) might establish the best positioning for his product, indicating whether it should be publicly interpreted as a luxury addition to a classy home or a health aid for asthmatic kids in any home.

Questions about the method of delivery would have to be worked out with people who understand the costs and constraints of the transport business.

Questions about advertising would have to be discussed with an ad agency. A public relations company would have to be pulled in to look at the public relations aspect of the problem, and perhaps a merchandiser consulted too.

When bringing your list of questions to a professional, remember one small thing. Let us whisper it in your ear, because, you see, we work for one of the consultancies you might visit, and we therefore seem to be cutting off our nose to spite our face. Here goes, anyway. *Ask an ad agency or a PR agency or a merchandiser if they think you need their services and they will always find a reason for the affirmative.* (Wild cries from friends and fellow professionals of Unfair, Unfair!) Our italics frame a generalisation, and like all generalisations, it has its exceptions, not least the fact that some PR agencies may be tied into advertising agencies and so you may approach one and they may say, honestly, that you don't need their services, but they effortlessly pass you on to the next arm of their corporate octopus. Some of the longer established consultancies are extra honest, partly because they are naturally honest, (yeah, well, some things authors have to say), partly because they're doing well enough not to bust a gizzard running after every bit of business that offers, and partly because they know that if they bend your real needs to fit what they can provide in the way of service, the twain may not meet and you may not in the final roundup be a happy customer. But hang on to the generalisation anyway. Keep your eye on your objective, which is to be your own boss, not to have a fabulous marketing plan informed by state of the art market research and back-lit by stunning advertising, PR and merchandising elements which cost you a fortune and take eons to complete.

Since generalisations are flying, let's add another. *Common sense, keeping your eyes open and asking a lot of stupid questions can turn a layperson into a great marketing expert.* (Add qualifications to taste.) Marketing, over the past thirty years, has become a huge science with a language all to itself and experts who can tell you the hidden significance of a millimetre of yellow border on a poster or diagnose and categorise your company as inward-looking—if you have developed and made a new stopper for soft drink bottles and now want to sell it—or outward looking—if instead of just trying to sell corks, you have committed yourself to the solution of customers' de-fizzed drink problem. (Outward looking, according to currently received wisdom, is the only way to be. Hmmm.)

Encountering a marketing professional can be a stimulating and extremely profitable session. It can also be a daunting bore. And sometimes it doesn't work.

If you're too young to remember Guinness Light, let us tell you about Guinness Light. Guinness Light was as it sounds. A lighter coloured, lighter textured version of Guinness Stout. The time was right. People were becoming more aware of healthy eating and drinking. "Lifestyle" was becoming a fashion. The core product had such a great image that it could be extended to take in variations, as Coke did with Cherry and Diet Cokes. Oh, sure, there would be reaction from the traditionalists, but the statistics showed marvellous new openings and, let's face it, the traditionalists might whinge that someone had dreamed up a pasty-faced version of their black favourite, but they'd go on drinking that black favourite, so let's not worry too much about their reaction. The whole campaign was picture perfect. The TV advertising was marvellous—strongly visual. Left you with the memory of bright cheery yellows and the defiant slogan "They said it couldn't be done." All the additional bits and pieces that add up both to good marketing and good merchandising were in position. Enough money was committed to ensure that this bright happy message would be repeated often enough to reach the target audience frequently enough to make a remembered impact. Within a couple of weeks, "They said it couldn't be done" was the tag line to a million ad libs. Within a couple of months, the word was out on how bad the Guinness Light sales were, and the line was amended to read "They said it couldn't be done, and boy, were they right..."

There are no guarantees in marketing, and the best marketing team in the world cannot make people buy something they really don't like, want or need.

But if you're trying to lay down a good marketing foundation for your product or service, don't miss out on the following hundred tips on doing it right:

Marketing Means You Look at Every Point Where You and Your Customers Meet

Many years ago, Jim Ward, Professor of Marketing at University College Galway, paid a friendly visit to Carr Communications, the communications and training consultancy in Dundrum, Dublin, where the two authors of this book are employed. As he prepared to drive his snazzy car away at the end of the visit, he nodded towards the potholes in our driveway. "Not great marketing," he said mildly.

We dropped to our knees and began to fill the potholes by bare hand. We also learned a basic lesson about marketing; at any point where your customers encounter you, they should like what they encounter. Even if you provide a great service, breaking a customer's back axle on his way to reach you may mean that his memories of the encounter are less than warm and that he will not return for more of the same.

Marketing Is Helped by a Good Name and a Logo That Makes a Statement. And a Colour to Match

A great name, trademark and colour or colours can at a glance establish your company and attract customers to it. This doesn't have to be a major expenditure, either. Some of the most creative artists, when it comes to designing logos, are not part of monolithic and expensive design houses, but loners or part of a two-person operation. Small businesses should support other small businesses, so go and look for the hungry talented starter.

Market by Doing Your Own Spot Checking

Be your own customer. As you arrive at your shop, try to see it as a first time customer would. Make phone calls to see how your staff receive them, or if your voice is too identifiable, get your mother or your aunt to make the calls.

Market through Publicity in the Right Place

Seeing your face in the paper is a great thrill. If it's a paper that doesn't reach your particular audience, it is no more than a great thrill. An interesting example of this principle in action is the company *Cashback*. They have offices at Dublin and Shannon

Airports and you'll see their stickers on the windows of retailers and department stores right around Ireland. What they offer is a system whereby visitors to this country can get their VAT refunded as they depart the country, if they've kept the right receipts. *Cashback* needs very little publicity for marketing purposes in Ireland. A certain level of awareness may be a good thing, so that retailers will feel they should be part of the *Cashback* network, but the real customer is the visitor from overseas who plans to buy a few costly items when on holiday in Ireland, and the appropriate timing is before the visitor reaches this country, so that from the word "go" they are looking out for the *Casback* logo at the entrance to premises they plan to patronise. So media which reach those visitors at home before they depart are of some significance, whether these are their local newspapers in Ohio or wherever, or the giveaway publications available from their travel agent. In-flight magazines may also be relevant. Mentions in the patter of tour guides thereafter may be more important than stories in Irish papers, because not that many tourists take time to browse through national newspapers when they are in mid-vacation.

Make Your Business Card a Working Business Card

Put a slogan on it. Or your hours of availability. Or a description of your business. Make it earn its keep.

Market by Staying Open Later Or Opening Earlier

Longer hours or different hours are oddly attractive. If you're a service industry and someone needs you on a day when you're already booked, offer to see the client at 6 in the morning. Even if that doesn't suit, the client will be happy you were prepared to go to such trouble to meet their needs.

Only Advertise If You Need to

Our own firm has never advertised and does not, at the present time, have an advertising budget. We do have publications, such as brochures, but word of mouth is where most of our business comes from, so that marketing emphasis must be on making sure the word from the mouth of our customers to the ear of potential customers is a happy one.

Help Your Own People to See Themselves as Marketers

Supermarket supremo Fergal Quinn is very good at personal PR. He is accessible to journalists and facilitates them when they're putting stories together. But, ultimately, he says that when customers go into Superquinn, the company is represented to them, not by their memory of the last thing they read about him, but by the person who serves them at the deli, or gives them information at the kiosk or hands them their change at the checkout. So these are the important marketing people for Superquinn, and must be both aware of the responsibility and trained in the skills necessary to deliver on it.

Use the Approach That's Appropriate for the Product—and for Your Company

Putting leaflets under windscreen wipers in the parking lot of a local shopping centre may be quite a good method of alerting people to a new tool-hire service. Especially if the leaflet carries a reduced price introductory coupon. Selling the concept of the local crematorium that way might be less successful. Similarly, selling through FAX shots is considered acceptable if you are offering something like an office catering service or business travel cheapo tickets, but classy operations selling expensive products or services are very wary of FAX as a marketing device, because of their feeling that it in some way is an invasion of corporate privacy.

Market—Don't Economise on Paper

Remember the point about looking at every interface? Cheapo paper and a tatty brochure filled with misprints do no favours for anybody's business.

Market by Finding Your Point of Differentiation

Imagine this. You knock on the door to sell your product, and the woman who answers looks over your shoulder. "See them?" she asks. You look, and there are eight people, all clean and tidy and wearing ingratiating smiles, and all carrying a product which is very like what you are selling. You turn back to the woman. "They're all selling one," she says. "Why should I buy yours? At that stage, you have to be able to dance up and down yelling one of these sort of responses:

- "Mine's the cheapest!"

- "Mine's the only one with a guarantee!"

- "Mine's the only one that can be tailored to fit your elbow/loo/hob/stairs."

- "Mine's the only one in pink." (Yellow, green or dotted.)

- "Mine's the only one approved by doctors."

- "Mine's the only one that has got sixty extra points for 700 kids doing the Leaving Cert in a Garda-supervised test run."

- "Mine's the only one Gay mentioned on the radio as being worth the money—hold on till I play you the tape!"

- "Mine's the only one that holds its retail value."

- "Mine's the one you get a free ticket to the big rock concert with."

- "Mine's the only one you get to taste before you buy." (This last was the way Debbi Fields started. Mrs Fields is a woman who has spread chocolate chip cookie shops in their hundreds right across America, in spite of the predictions of people who said that cookies or biscuits, as we would call them, are mass production items and people prefer them crisp. Mrs Fields produced individually crafted bumpy cookies which were moist and soft, chopped them up into quarters, and stood around the shopping mall with chopped chunks of cookie on a saucer, offering the chunks free of charge as samples to passersby. Once they had experienced a soft buttery cookie, people became converts and she was on her way to becoming a multi-millionaire.)

Repeat Your Message

People, these days, are drowning in information. It's cominatcha from everywhere. Radio, TV, hoardings, newspapers, magazines, FAXes, phone calls, bleeps and mobile phones. So a lot of what is transmitted gets lost in the aural and visual static. (Test it yourself. Sit beside a man watching an international rugby match in which his own country is playing, at a point when there is about ten minutes left in the game, and the score is even. As the players all crouch down into that obscure moving turtle shape, ask the man watching what was the last ad he saw when the TV camera took in the perimeter fencing. If he acknowledges that you spoke, he is likely to a) tell you to get lost, and b) to ask testily *what* ad, for Chrissake? He has not registered any advertisement at all, even though the bill to the client company for putting an ad in the background to the play, where a TV camera will pan over it, is enormous. Indeed, the same man may never listen to the radio, because he is a classical music freak and plays CDs in his car player, so he misses radio ads. He may miss TV most of the time because he works late, so commercials for the most part pass him by. But if the ad campaign is repeated enough, he will gradually catch some of the exposures of the commercial or the slogan, and become peripherally aware of what is being sold. Repetition in this noisy, over-informed world, is vital. It is generally believed that one of the reasons Michael Dukakis failed in his campaign to be President of the US was because he never learned the value of repetition. If his opponent accused him of something, he would deny it in a speech, and that, as far as he was concerned, was an end to it. Similarly, he would make some stunning appeal to a group of voters and would be puzzled when his campaign management wanted him to articulate the same point again and again. He had made his point, why should he keep hammering it? Unfortunately for Dukakis, the reality is that the audience for messages is not standing by with a notebook in hand ready to write down and learn off a signal which is sent to them once only. The audience for messages, as Yeats observed, has itself "a little round of deeds and days" about which to be preoccupied, and a message that's going to remain in their head has to be insinuated a lot more than once.

Find Time to Market

When you invent something or come from the production side of an industry, you tend to the frame of mind which waves a dismissive hand at marketing and says "let *them* do that." Which may result in your marketing department or your bought-in marketing professionals trying to sell something they don't quite understand to a market they shouldn't be trying to reach. There should be no segregation. As a boss, you are not slumming it if you become integral to the marketing effort. You should be integral to the marketing of your product or service, and your staff should know that.

Marketing Means Abandoning Things That Don't Work

That does not mean that because the boss's husband doesn't like the radio commercial, it gets ditched. It does mean that after an appropriate period, if it can be shown indisputably that, say, a certain kind of mail-shot has no payoff, it should be allowed to die. The military maxim is that you should never reinforce failure. Small businesses, however, are often so conscious of the awful cost of everything that when one aspect of marketing fails, they feel so guilty over having put X amount of money into it that they think maybe if they added Y amount of money they could make the X pay off. Now, repeat after me: *I will admit but not reinforce failure.*

Marketing Means Controlling Expenditure

Every new business encounters this situation. You have developed a detailed marketing plan and a budget to match. Marketing starts. The first people it reaches are not the people who will buy something from you, but the people who want to sell something to you. Out of the woodwork come all of the marketing people working for other enterprises. The ad salespeople for newspapers and magazines, who assure you that if you take an ad in their upcoming supplement it will pull in new customers you never dreamed you could reach. The guy who has dreamed up a little laminated card carrying details of the most important businesses in your area, inclusion in which, he assures you, will set you up for life. The local charity, which promises you that a sponsorship of a couple of thousand quid will get you a mention in their literature for the next three hundred years and let all potential customers know that you are a Caring Company. Make your marketing budget stick, because if it doesn't, there are no lengths to which it will not expand, with very little in the way of measurable payoff.

Patronage Is Different from Sponsorship and Don't Do It

Patronage is where a company sponsors some person or event which is of no value to the company's bottom line. Sponsorship is where there is a direct beneficial link. Patronage is a self-indulgent form of rich company charity no start-up company can afford.

Marketing is Never Sloppy

If your response time in answering letters is too slow, the sloppiness will be referred by potential clients to your entire business. ("Gawd, if they're that slow in answering a simple letter, I'd hate to be waiting for them to deliver a consignment...")

Make Your Marketing Bullet-Proof

Never make a claim that can't be substantiated, because someone will either sue you or create a media stink.

Be Wary of Backhanders

There are some businesses where getting an order can involve an expectation on the part of the purchaser that you will, in some way "see him right." This is ethically wrong. This is also organisationally wrong, because low morale often ensues, due to staff realisation that it isn't the value of what they are producing which is recognised in a big sale, but the size of the bribe. There are always enough straight customers out there to allow you to make a legit living.

Market What the Customer Likes in Your Product, Not What *You* Like

What do happy customers say when they talk about your product or service? It doesn't always match what you personally value in that product or service—but it is probably closer to what will help you sell. Marketing is not self-stroking or re-inforcement of one's own values. It is turning one's product around so that its most immediately likeable aspect is squarely facing the new customer.

Market by the Rules

There are some kinds of ads that you can't broadcast, because they infringe some rules of the broadcasting organisations. There are some words which will pull every activist group in the country down around your ears. Yes, we hear you say, but our ad agency will take care of that. Remember what we said about being an integral part of marketing? Don't slough that responsibility off onto your ad agency. It may not work. Get from the Advertising Standards Authority its specifications and have a look at the sort of ads that have had to be withdrawn. Some ad agency thought up those ads—but some business like yours paid for them and then probably had to pay for the making of another ad to replace the one which was taken off.

Market with an Understandable Name

If you have an unpronounceable name that's difficult to convey over a phone and that looks threatening in print, think twice about using it as the title for your firm. Why should customers make the effort and embarrass themselves?

Market through Your Location

Even if you're not a high street operation your premises should, to any visitor, sum up your operation. A customer might want to see your production facilities before placing a big order. A photographer might want to take a picture for a business magazine. Most important of all, if you want your staff to be proud of what they do and what they produce it will greatly help if they like the look of the place in which they work. The busiest, noisiest factory can be made cheerful and—in factory terms—tidy. The most cramped starter premises can be turned into a small hive of happy activity.

Market through Individuality

When a customer rings you to query a particular problem and, when his worries have been eliminated, says "I knew *your* company would never do that particular thing," or "I knew *your* company would never take that approach," you have marketed your unique and individual standards well. Make sure your customers know what you stand for—and what you don't stand for.

Market through Speed

Joe Bloggs rings your company and wants a proposal. A good proposal a week from now is satisfactory. A good proposal delivered by hand tomorrow may be *noticeably* satisfactory.

Market through Understanding of the Customer's Individuality

Never respond to an individual query with a mass produced reply. Nobody in the world is pleased with a form letter which has their name scribbled in at the top. Yes, you will have template answers in your word processor, because much of the information you will want to send to potential customers will be standard, but train yourself and your people to pose as many questions as they can dream up when that potential customer makes their first call, because the better you understand a customer's business, the tighter can your tailored response be to their needs, and the quicker a real relationship is set up. Nobody wants to think of themselves as just a blob like six million other blobs. Each of us is an individual to ourselves, and just as you think of your own business as unique and especially interesting, so do most other bosses.

Never Think of Marketing as Being the Same as Advertising

A bugler can make a big noise, but if a varied, well-equipped and highly motivated army isn't in there behind him, he loses the war tunefully and fast.

Marketing Is Follow Up

Anyone can sell something once. A customer is a great asset. But a loyal customer is an invaluable asset, and you create loyal customers by following up.

Honest Marketing Does Not Steal Ideas

(It adapts pretty creatively, though. On occasion.)

Good Marketing Is Not about Tinkering

Ad agencies rightly hate the client who really, really likes the campaign, and approves it, but who would prefer if it wasn't a bus-stop the teenager was seen at, and who would prefer if the word "super', followed, rather than preceded, the word "mega" and would like the full name and address of the company given perhaps in the bottom left hand corner. Bosses should throw the whole thing out, but not tinker with detail about which they may lack insight and experience.

Marketing Means Repeating the Name

If you think we made this point before, you're wrong. We said the message bears virtually endless repetition. But repeating the message might mean that you sell a concept; people might get to like the idea of little bells on their shoes. If it isn't your bells that they buy, however, you have not only done half the job, but you've done the wrong half. You have sent business to your competitors. Remember that at cocktail and other parties, when people are introduced, they very rarely learn each other's names immediately. Someone always has to do retrospective muttering to the effect that "you know that blonde girl you introduced me to—over there in the pink—right. What's her name again?" Moral? Even when it's in our best interests, we don't learn names. So if someone is selling us something, they'd better make sure we learn their name. Through repetition.

Market by Never Blaming the Customers

Every now and again, we go to a marketing seminar where someone makes a presentation which effectively says "The general public were too stupid, lazy or lacking in class to buy this product." Maybe. But if you believe your business failed for one of those reasons, keep it to yourself. You might want to start again at some stage, and if you have insulted the audience, they don't usually welcome you for an encore.

Market by Never Trying to Prove the Customer Wrong

It is mind-blowing the number of companies which, when a complaint is made or a customer prefers the product of a competitor, will go to considerable trouble to prove to the customer that he or she is wrong. It can be done. It rarely motivates the customer to buy. Provable egg on one's face is a cosmetic most of us can live without.

Please Market Inclusively

If you're commissioning ads, talk to your ad agency about making the images inclusive, rather than exclusive. In other words, there are those of us out here who are old or in some way disabled, and we tend to get left out of the happy world portrayed in ads. Not in America, we don't tend to get left out. McDonald's hamburger joints, in the States, will feature old customers. Nike shoes will show a wheelchair athlete. Nissan cars will feature a buyer who happens to be in a wheelchair. *You* could be the leader in Ireland in this good trend.

Market for the Long Term

A marketing campaign which centres on a personality may cause problems in the long term, for the personality or for the company which is tied to the personality, and if you are a small company, you need to think very carefully before you hitch your wagon to an individual, no matter how appropriate that individual seems to be as a figurehead for your product or service. The Maurice Pratt approach to advertising is greatly helped, for Quinnsworth, by the fact that Maurice Pratt is Marketing Director for that company and so has an identification with them that doesn't have to be pretended. On the other hand, it can be assumed that at some point Maurice Pratt might like a private life and an existence other than his television existence. No doubt Quinnsworth have a long-term marketing strategy to take in that eventuality. Make sure you think in the same extended way.

Marketing Is Not about Saying Bad Things about Competitors

Quite often, a potential client will test the waters before committing himself to a contract by asking you about your competitors. Praise them by identifying something about their operation you particularly admire. Or smile and tell the client that he can't seriously expect you to fill him in on your competition. Don't bad-mouth them. Bad-mouthing them says much more about you than it says about them and what it says is negative.

Marketing Is Sometimes about Filling Forms

A couple of the multi-nationals in Ireland do not let you come and present to them and bowl them over, knock their socks off and curl their hair with excitement at what you have to offer, because they realise that a great presentation or sales pitch does not always add up to delivery of a great end result. So they send you a twenty-page questionnaire to fill up. It goes against your grain, and the inclination is to lash through it and fling it back with a brochure. Don't. Spend time and care on it, because it could result in you being awarded "Vendor Status," which means that every department in that multinational will favour you when it comes to follow-up orders. Read through the questionnaire very carefully, because if you start to answer without having the full picture, you may assume that question three means what question seven in fact means. If the verbiage confuses you, ring up and seek clarification from someone—it will underline your interest in the contract and it will make someone in their HQ remember your name.

Marketing Is Not Whinging

Small business are at the mercy of all sorts of uncontrollable external factors, and there is always an urge to go out and tell people about how those factors are doing you no end of harm. It doesn't move goods off shelves. People almost never buy out of sympathy. Worse, it may give you an image as a whinger, which is not a good thing to have. Many of our most vulnerable small business in this country are farms. They are subject to weather, international regulation, environmental activists, pressure from imported goods, rises in interest levels and increases in fuel prices. Inevitably, they whinge. Thus they are seen as whingers. Often unfairly. But when has sympathy for the farming community ever seriously motivated your personal purchase of a cabbage?

Marketing Wins on Percentages

Cold call and telephone selling is something you would not wish on your worst enemy, because both have such a low success rate. If you're selling something, then it might take one hundred refusals, rejections and downright rude dollops of responsive abuse before you make ten sales. Which is why these areas have such a high staff turnover. People can't stand the rejection, can't cope with the failure. The people who stay doing this kind of work for years and who make money on it have come to terms with one simple fact about marketing; each sale is like one white brick in a wall mainly made up of red bricks. But you could never make the wall without the red bricks. What you need to do is mooch around to find out what the predictable percentage is on whatever marketing you're doing. Not so long ago, we were consulted by a company which was very disappointed because it only got a forty per cent return on a major mailshot. All we could do was gape and laugh. Gape because forty per cent was the highest return we had ever heard accruing to this kind of mailshot (five per cent would have been fine and dandy) and laugh because not only were the company wrong to come to us to show them what they were doing wrong, they should probably have been out giving lessons in how to do mailshots phenomenally *right*!

Marketing Is Solidarity

If a customer rings to complain about the way Sue talked to her on the phone, apologise for the offence immediately and say it's not part of your company style. Make the customer feel mollified, even if it means making a special arrangement to deliver something early or at a discount, but don't ever make a customer feel mollified by saying nasty things about your own staff. Deal with that matter privately, and you will have some hope of turning Sue into part of the company's marketing team, rather than a permanently de-motivated fifth columnist.

Market to Your Customers, Not to Marketing Buffs

Marketing buffs love marketing approaches which are innovative and creative and iconoclastic. Marketing buffs love advertising which is witty, verbally clever and visually artistic. None of those things necessarily sell your product. In one corner is your product, or service. In another corner is the customer. Your job is getting them together, not entertaining the uninvolved bystanders.

Market Past "No"

Never strike a customer off your list. The buyer who turns you down on this occasion may be retired in three months' time. The supplier who won the order may not satisfy their expectations. Or they may decide that they don't like to be dependent on one single supplier. So go back. Go back as cheerfully as you went the first time.

Market Using Names

Remember people's names and specifications. (Not personal specifications, unless you're a politician, in which case the state of the voter's bad back and the unemployment levels of his children may be relevant to your sales pitch.) No, before you skip on, stick with us for a moment. Remember the names and specifications in writing if at all possible, so that when you go back to that company in three months time, you remember it was Terry Pilchard you talked to, and you further remember that he said his priorities were choice of colour and cost.

Market to Current Realities

When in Yuppieland, do not make like a hippie leftover from the Sixties. Hang on to your own values by all means, but never project them as salespoints to a market that doesn't share them.

Market Your Strengths, Not Your Weaknesses

So the salesman is explaining his business, and the

customer says "Oh, you've only got six people working in that company?" and the salesman says that he assures the customer on his personal word that the small size of his company would not be allowed in any way to inconvenience the customer. The customer says yeah, right, and gets the skids under the salesman quicker than quick. Instead, the salesman should have said something like "Yeah, that's one of the things the X company manager said he particularly liked about us—when he rings up, he always talks to someone who knows him and his company. He doesn't get passed from hand to hand the way larger companies sometimes do. Oh, and the other thing I should mention is that our size helps us do more personalised jobs. You know you need a jacket personalised for your exhibition, but you only need twelve of them? Well a larger company would either turn you away or cost you the earth, but we're small and hungry, and we've been working on the idea, and here's our sketch of what we think it should look like, and here's the costing..."

Market by Learning from Failure

You didn't get the order. End of story. Except that it should *not* be end of story. You ring up the guy you dealt with you and say "Roger, we didn't get your order. Help me to make sure we don't make the same mistake again—what was it that made you decide against us?" Sometimes they won't tell you. Sometimes they will. When they do, the lost order may be due to something you can neither control nor change. But it just might be due to something you never thought about or could change, thereby improving your chances next time around.

Market Briefly

Control your desire to say everything about your product, its manufacturing process, your company history, your personal probity. Make the point the customer cares about, then shut up.

Marketing is about Over-Reacting to Customer Complaint

Never brush aside a complaint. The complaint that gets expressed is the exception, but it isn't a bird alone. The statistics vary, but it has been estimated that for every complaint which is actually verbalised, there are at least twenty unexpressed. But the person who does not express a complaint to you is precisely the person who goes away and expresses it to eight other people, thus doing an extremely effective anti-marketing job for your company. So when you get a complaint, don't tell the person nobody has ever complained about that before. Listen. Cherish the complainer. Solve the problem. Make them feel better (and sometimes just solving the problem doesn't do that, because they have been so annoyed). Prevent it ever happening again. In a small company, there's often no system for complaints, and a complainer fobbed off at a low level is a very aggravated complainer. So talk to your people about how to handle complaints, and make yourself available if need be to get back to the complainer, because, in the commercial world, a problem solved is not a problem halved, it is a problem turned into a marketing advantage. Problem-owning customers who meet with respect, openness and corrective action are customers for life.

Market through Contacts and Associations

You know what they say about joining an association or attending a conference? "It's not that you learn that much or gain that much, but you do make contacts, and you never know when they'll turn out to be useful." This is true, but should not be over-stated as a benefit to a start-up company. The Marketing Manager or Boss who gets tickled with the idea of becoming President of the Such and Such Association is a person who may lose contact with his main objective: to make a success of the business. The warm support of your peers can be a pleasing, profitless seduction.

Market through Livery

Brightly matched cars all carrying your company imprint and a tag line indicating what business you do can be a good marketing device. But only if your staff are happy to drive the cars. If they're hiding them around the back of car parks rather than have to answer questions about them, it's counter-productive. It suits some businesses, doesn't suit others.

Market through Incentive

Every staff member who creates a contact or brings in, no matter how accidentally, a sale, should be rewarded for it. By corollary, as soon as they know they *will* be rewarded for it, quite surprising staff members get down to serious selling.

Market around Your Accountant

Accountants get jittery when marketing is the question, because accountants live on predictables and on cost-justification, and marketing is never either predictable in its results nor cost-justifiable. The old crack about fifty per cent of every marketing budget being wasted, but nobody knowing *which* fifty per cent, is still true. So market around your accountant and don't give him/her a veto.

Market Opportunistically

When Ireland got as far as it did in the last World Cup, a lot of opportunistic marketing by small operators made them a lot of money. Some of the cleverest T-shirts ever designed surfaced overnight after particular matches. The entrepreneurs behind these efforts were following in a fine tradition: Levi Strauss jeans started off when a German immigrant during the California Gold Rush overestimated the amount of tent canvas the market could bear, and had to figure out something else to do with the cloth. Tough working trousers seemed a fair bet, and that was the genesis of a legend.

Market Alphabetically

Directories and media which run classified ads will tell you that the names appearing early on in a list are the first to be contacted by people who want to buy something. That's great if your name occurs high up in the alphabet, but it's tough on people with names like Stephenson and Prone, which appear way down the alphabet and whose parents didn't have the wit to give them first names like Amy or Amanda. When you're planning a name for your company or product, it may be worth your while getting up there in the A team. (If you sell through the classifieds, find a way of describing your product so that your advertising copy begins with an A. Or a B if you're really pushed.)

Market through Quality

Talk to the Irish Quality Control Association to see if your product or process merits the Quality Mark. It's an extra claim, validated by a third party, which can differentiate you from your competitors.

Market through Being Unique

"Unique" can be achieved in all sorts of ways. It always attracts notice—and customers. As we go to press, stories are appearing in magazines of two women in Donegal living a life free of modern conveniences like electricity. They wear Victorian dreess and sell gowns of the same style. They attract attention and customers by their uniqueness.

Market through Being Small

Avis did it when they were Number Two as car rental company. They said "Hey, we're number two, so we try harder." What is small attracts sympathy and support. Can you ever remember anyone rooting for Goliath?

Market through Being New

Talk about your fresh ideas. Your young, enthusiastic staff. Your state-of-the-art equipment. New, to the sceptic, means unproven and untried. But sold hard enough, it can carry completely positive connotations.

Market through Mentions

If you cannot afford to hire professionals to do your PR for you, then (this is a plug, but we have no choice) buy the best book available on how to do your own publicity, which is appropriately titled *Do Your Own Publicity*. It's by Terry Prone. If you can't find it in your local bookshop, send £10.99 inclusive of post and packaging to Poolbeg. Remember, a free mention in someone's column may sell more of your product than a purchased advertisement.

Market by Reminder

The pharmaceutical companies worked out a long time ago that sending a representative to a doctor to give the doctor information about a branded drug was only part of the marketing task. Advertising was another part, but the focal point was that when the doctor decided that the treatment required by a patient's symptoms was of a particular kind, the chemical company needed the doctor to remember their brand name of medicine fitting into that chemical configuration. So they developed the desk reminder to a fine art. Next time you visit your GP, count the number of objects on his or her desk which carry a pharmaceutical company's brand name or the brand name of a single product or pill. There are likely to be pens, tongue depressors, timing devices, calendars, memo pads, blotters and a whole lot more. What you can learn from the pharmaceutical companies is that if you are selling a business-related product, then you must find a way of getting a reminder about that product onto the desk with a target. Preferably in a form which is not in itself a cliché (like a pen).

Market through Reference

"We build great factories," is not as good a claim as "We've just built a great factory for X, the household name prestigious makers of Y, and they think it's the best factory they've ever occupied and would be only too happy to have you visit it." Try to create "reference sites," customers or locations which show previous work you've done and indicate customer satisfaction with that work. Third party testimonial to your worth is immeasurably more useful than first person assertion.

Market by Making It Easy to Get to Your Premises

If you're slightly off the beaten track, don't give customers a problem in finding you because they just might say the hell with it and go buy a pint. Find ways of putting up signposts to guide them to you. In a shared building, make sure that every available noticeboard has a permanent indicator of where you are, rather than a pencilled one. Should you ever take a room in a hotel to demonstrate your products or services, make sure that your name is properly spelled on their little blackboard type notifier in the lobby and that the correct number is alongside it. Put maps on the reverse of your business card or your compliment slip, and have your receptionist geared to tell people what are the best buses, DART stations or other methods of reaching you.

Market by Topicality

When will women buy cosmetics lacking a glamorous brand name, presented in relentlessly ordinary plastic bottles and bereft of the elegant packaging normally associated with cosmetic purchases? When these products are environmentally friendly and not tested on animals. There are few cities these days which don't have a Body Shop or its equivalent. If your product can be marketed in such a way that it scratches a topical itch (like Body Shop's Products), market it in that way.

Market by Piggyback

Someone else is promoting something by means of a competition. Suggest your product to the promoter as a focus for the competition. Have a look at your ESB bill the next time it comes in. It will probably have a competition for which you qualify by paying your bill quickly, and the prizes will start with a motor car and work down to kitchen gadgets. Many people will be attracted to enter by the colour pictures of the car and the gadgets, and when they don't win, will still remember the brand names of the items feature. Many people will not bother to enter, but will still register the name.

Market by Personally Monitoring Your Merchandising

Example. One of the most successful recent product developments in Ireland. A household product which had never been produced here—always imported. So an Irish company began to make it and sell it. The Marketing Director handed over the merchandising to a specialist company, which placed the product on the shelves, made sure nobody was left without it for more than a few hours, and put up little counter stickers and flags to draw shoppers' attention to it. "They did very well," she told us. "But I never handed it totally over to them. Once a week I would go out and spend the day touring shops at random, and every time I found our product pushed in behind someone else's, or not properly displayed, I either went to work right there and then to fix it, or I rang them and created hell."

Market by Mail # 1

Because Ireland is geographically small, we have never grown a mail order industry like the United States, where companies like Sears, Roebuck would ship you anything from a pair of jeans to a tractor, if you lived in an outlying area, and where going through the catalogues of mail-order houses was a pleasant way to spend a winter's evening. We are beginning to have mail-order businesses here now, and if you manufacture something which you believe fits into the kind of range they sell, have a word with the producer of the catalogue. If you have a product you would like to sell in the United States, then mail order is one of the methods you should consider. If a big mail order house decides to sell your product, it can take over the marketing problem and publicise the item right across the nation. All you have to do is make sure the volume and quality of the product stay right.

Market by Mail # 2

An Post have been knocking themselves out to prove that they are good business partners, and they have all sorts of cheaper ways in which you can market in bulk, including a cassette post system which is very useful. (See Market by Cassette, below). Talk to them.

Market by Mail # 3

Obviously the purpose of marketing by mail is to sell your product or service. There is no such thing as an average response rate, so you will have to be sure that you are able to meet the demand for your product or service generated from your mailshot. Perhaps the best way to gauge the likely response is to test-market your mailing with a small number and then carry out your actual mailing at a level allowing you to meet the demand as forecast by responses to your test mailing.

It is most important for your credibility with your customers that you fulfil their requests within a reasonable period. Be sure you have the staff and stock to meet demand. It would be a shame to spoil a good marketing campaign by being too successful!

Market by Mail # 4

So who do you mail to?

You probably already have a list of your own customers and they are the ones who are most likely to do future business with you. However, you may be looking for fresh fields, and there are many ways to obtain lists which may help you find new customers. Professional bodies and associations keep lists of their members and may be willing to give or sell you that list. Publications have lists of subscribers and specialist list owners compile lists of businesses and individuals specifically to allow marketing by mail. For instance *Business & Finance* annually publish a list of Ireland's top companies and you can either obtain that from a back copy of the publication of purchase the list as software from them. Other publications such as *Kompass Business Information Register of Irish Industry and Commerce* are also very useful.

Do you need lists? An Post offers an unaddressed mailing service, so if you wish to market in a particular area you can cover every household or business in that chosen area without even addressing the envelopes.

Market by Mail # 5

If marketing by mail is an area you want to enter or one which you think may help you to sell your product or service, perhaps the soundest advice we could give is to use An Post's service. Not only does An Post publish a brochure for each of the services it offers to mail-marketers, but its salesforce offers a free consultancy service. It will help you along the road to marketing your product or service by mail.

Market by Cassette

People put brochures away, intending to read them. Sometime. The same people may be surprised to receive an audio cassette from you, and, because business people often have cassette machines in their cars, may click it in and listen to it. That's one-to-one marketing at its best, and the production of a high quality audio cassette is quite cheap. As is An Post's Cassette Post Scheme.

Market by Early Morning Phone

Many small new businesses find that because their name is not known, they have difficulty getting to major decision makers in large companies or state sponsored bodies. They run into the fence. A hint. Telephone the company before normal starting time. The CEO just may be there, because a lot of them start early. But his or her secretary may *not* be there, and—keep those fingers crossed—you could get through to them.

Market by Free Sample

We hate those little stands you fall over in super-markets these days, where a bright-faced woman is trying to interest passing adults in some diced food product on a stick. (The toddlers are fighting for this food product, but the woman is always hoping to reach the adult minding the toddler. Or *not* minding it, as the case may be.) However, we are told by producers that this method of introducing a food product is effective and we reluctantly pass this good news on to you, gentle reader.

Market by Solving the Customer's Problem

You see it every week in your local shop, if they have a "Community Noticeboard." Someone will stick up a notice saying they'll babysit or do ironing or give your teenager a grind in maths, and at the end of the notice is a little fringed section, where the amateur advertiser has written down their phone number four or five times, sideways, and then used a scissors to turn the numbered bits of paper into tear-off reminders. This is the marketer solving the customer's problem, the problem being that the person going into the supermarket doesn't have time, inclination or a pen to note a number, even if they would like to have that number. Think of ways of making easier the task of reaching you.

Market by Flier

Again, we hate them, but they seem to work, these loose print notifications which can be inserted into one of the freebie newspapers circulated in cities. This can be highly cost-effective if you can arrange to have it inserted only in that issue of the freebie which is delivered in the neighbourhood you want to reach.

Market by Credit Card

Some customers have become so used to credit cards that it is their preferred method of payment. Depending on your business, it may be worth talking to the credit card companies to see if you should be accredited with them.

Market by Specialist Publication

If your product is of use only to carpenters, there's not much point in advertising or seeking free publicity in a ballet magazine. Find out what is the appropriate trade magazine and the best way of getting into it.

Market to Special Interests

There is no such thing, any more, as "the General Public." Niche marketing is the buzz word. Would your product, at a special price, be of interest to older people? Would your product, packaged in a particular way, be of interest to younger people? Or people in a particular kind of house? Driving a particular kind of car?

Market with Respect

Create in your firm a corporate culture that doesn't see customers as an interruption of the more important task of administration, and don't allow, within your company, disrespectful terms for customers to become currency. They are customers, guests, clients or friends. Not "punters" or "guys in the front office" or "the old bag in the showroom." Market what you know about, market what you care about, to people you respect.

Market by Going the Extra Mile

Don't just solve a problem—over-solve it. Don't just
satisfy your customers, astonish them. One customer
saying to someone else "I can't get over them in Xs,
they really put themselves out to get me what I
wanted" is worth £ thousands in purchased advertising. Give clients better value than they expect to
deserve and they'll return the compliment.

Market Positively

Not "we're not open on Saturday afternoon." Instead
try "we're open all morning on Saturday."

Market Even in Crowds

If three people are lined up, deal with the one in
front of you, but talk to the others and assure them
of your concern at their delay. Don't ignore them.
Ditto with phone callers.

Market to a Clearly Valued Customer

The story goes that one irritated customer once told
a surly garage mechanic "Listen, mister, you've got
it wrong. To this company, you're overhead. *I'm*
profit!" How true those words are, even today...

Market on Your Off Days

You never get a second chance to make a first
impression.

Market Manageable Expectations

Not so long ago, a Managing Director of a high-tech company came to Carr Communications with an old problem: his salesmen were too good. They had been to one of those training schools where you're taught how to spruce yourself up while you shave in the morning (bit difficult for women, this), shake a customer's hand so warmly he's rattling broken finger bones for the rest of the day, and run him down, juggernaut-fashion, with a spiel which is heavy on the miracle, Harry, and light on facts. These spiel-burgers were moving product, all right. As the MD bluntly put it, they were "selling computers they didn't understand to customers whose needs they hadn't established." The end result was a constantly moving bag of disappointed expectations. Never set up expectations larger than you can deliver if you plan on any future with the client.

Market through Sales Reps, Not Robots

(See above.) Some training turns out sales reps who don't listen to the customers, don't know their own product in any real way and do not satisfactorily represent their company. Instead they are good at "maintaining four eye contact," at "feedback" (meaning the apparent flattery of repeating back to the customer what the customer has just said), and at "mirroring." The last is a trick whereby you time your breathing with that of the customer, stand the way he or she does, and speak at his rate and in the same tone of voice. "Mirroring" is widely peddled as the last word in empathic behaviour, and as a guarantee that the customer will like the seller, because (goes the argument) don't we all like people who are like us? This sort of marketing puts the customer on edge and puts locks on wallets. Get *real*. And make sure your sales reps get real, too.

Market Not by Hard-Sell But by Easy Buy

People—particularly Irish people—hate to feel they're being *sold* something. Don't do a song and dance. Just remove the obstacles which prevent someone from buying.

Market to Keep Your Existing Customers

Most businesses spend about 6 times more to attract new customers than they would have to spend to keep an existing one. Grapple existing customers to your heart with hoops of steel.

Market by Good Administration

One phone call, unreturned because, in your absence, the message taker didn't write it down or wrote down a wrong digit, can lose you £100 or £1,000 or £10,000.

Market by People

Avoid answering machines. OK at night, maybe, but during lunchtime? Have a human answer your phone, even if that human has to eat yogurt at their desk. If you must have an answering machine, take the time to record and re-record your message so that you end up sounding like you and sounding as if you care about the customer who's ringing. Check your messages and respond quickly.

Market by Meeting Impossible Deadlines

You've seen the cartoon. Everybody has. There are the three (or is it four) roundy little cartoon figures falling all over each other and onto the floor with laughter, under the question "You want it *when?*". Meeting an impossible deadline is a great way to endear yourself to a customer. But it costs extra.

Market to Customers You Really Want to Have

And, by corollary, resign accounts you no longer enjoy. This obviously applies to service industries. Let's put our own belief on the table: we are hungry to serve you. But we're not bought just by money. If you're a pain in the ass, then no matter what you pay us, we'll fire you. No, we're not making a mistake. We understand that we're the lowly consultants and you're the valued client. But the fact remains: if you're a pain in the ass, no money would persuade

239

us to work for you long term. (Suppliers have human rights, too.)

Market through the Contact List You Didn't Know You Had

Start writing down names of people you know. At random. Push yourself. Don't stop until you have 250. Now, can you sell any of those people something? Why not? You want to market to the big wide world but the people you know aren't good enough? Or is it that your product is not good enough for any of them? Get your head straight. From the moment you start up in business, write down the name, address and phone number of every contact. When you hit marketing problems, go through the list. You'll be surprised by what it will yield.

Market through Punctuality

If you value the business someone's giving you or thinking of giving you, never be late for a meeting— even if you have to arrive half an hour early and go for a walk around the block.

Don't Market by Pounding People with Logic

One of the good reasons for getting an ad agency to write publicity copy for you is that you may understand the claims it's legitimate to make on behalf of your product, but a third party can make those claims fly. Because customers are rarely attracted by relentless logic. People often buy emotionally and then reverse retrospectively rationalise their purchase.

Market without Too Many Options

A wealth of choices can confuse a customer into making no choice at all.

Market by Meaning It

If you don't believe in what you're saying (and selling) it'll show. Sooner or later.

Market by Knowing the Ethos of Your Overseas Country

One friend of ours spent a fortune on a brochure for a Moslem country in the Middle East. Got the language right. Got the business terms right. And decorated the text with light visuals of pretty women dressed in bright, culturally offensive gear. They didn't get the job. Surprise, surprise.

Market by Media

Media exposure can give your product or service an odd and sometimes spurious public status. The fact that your brand was mentioned in a TV programme, preferably a highly popular TV programme, can make it considerably more attractive to potential stockists. Which means that some entrepreneurs, mad for "a mention," approach programmes in quite the wrong way.

The *Late Late Show* once a year does a programme which features new inventions, start-up businesses, driving entrepreneurial individuals— and a level of competition between people in the audience which makes bare-fist boxing look gentle. Each and every member of that audience, it seems to the home viewer, has one thing and one thing only on his/her mind; attracting a camera, a microphone and Gay Byrne's attention long enough to blurt "I'm X and I'm from Y and I make Z." When the audience member decides to be very subtle and to be seen actually to contribute to the progress of the show, the audience member says something like, "I'm X and I'm from Y and I make Z and I totally agree with what the last speaker said."

Understandably, the researcher responsible, Brigid Ruane, tends to have problems getting past all of this relentless self-selling in order to create an entertaining show.

"Many of them start from a simple desire to be on the show, because they see the *Late Late Show* as the most powerful vehicle for their marketing message. They know that shops are much more likely to stock their product if it's got a mention on the programme."

The researcher starts from a different point of view. She is trying to structure a show amounting to something more than a tedious list of boasts, claims, names and addresses.

"I have spent until twelve at night with people who were appearing," she says wearily. "I have talked to them until I'm blue in the face. I think I've even offended some of them because I'm looking for what is interesting to the people at home, I'm looking for a novel product or an individual story that's worth telling, or, indeed, an inspiring story, and all any of them want is a quick mention. In the end of the day, I believe that everybody gains if the programme is entertainingly informative, encouraging, and inspiring for others."

Use an opportunity like the *Late Late Show* badly and while you can certainly claim, thereafter, that you were featured on the programme, that's an end to it. The following year, the programme people are likely to shrink from you as from a nasty infectious disease.

So before you lift the phone to Brigid Ruane with your query "Can you give us some coverage?" do your homework. Find what is off-beat or unusual or intriguing about your product. Establish that you're willing to talk about some of the disasters on the way to your success. On the phone and on the programme (if you're lucky enough to get a ticket) don't be crudely self-serving; try to solve the programmers' problems and try, above all, to offer something the viewers will find riveting.

Market through Failure

A distinguishing characteristic of successful entrepreneurs is that they don't recognise failure in the sense of acknowledging final disaster. They acknowledge mistakes, but see them as an inevitable part of onward progress, not as personal indictments or as setbacks. (Indeed, one of the annoying things about entrepreneurs who seem to have been born for it is that they will happily blame accountants or suppliers, and keep their own self esteem intact.) Entrepreneurs fail *towards* success. Or, as James Joyce said "a man of genius makes no mistakes. His errors are volitional and are the portals of discovery."

Appendix 1
Tax, PRSI, VAT and All Those Other Things

Tax

Ireland now has a self-assessment tax system for companies, self-employed people, partnerships—anyone who does not pay their tax under the PAYE (Pay As You Earn) system. The Revenue Commissioners have produced a booklet, *A Self-help Guide —Self Assessment Tax* which you can get through your local tax office or from self-assessment information telephone numbers

---

Self Assessment Information Phone Numbers

Athlone (0902) 92681	Letterkenny (074) 21299
Castlebar (094) 21344	Limerick (061) 31711
Cork (021) 966077	Sligo (071) 60322
Dublin (01) 689400	Thurles (0504) 21544
Dundalk (042) 32251	Tralee (066) 21844
Galway (091) 63041	Waterford (051) 73565
Kilkenny (074) 21299	Wexford (053) 23207

Effectively what happens is that companies must calculate and pay their tax within six months of the end of their accounting period. An accounting period is usually a one-year period. So if the company's year ends on 31 December, 1990 the company must calculate its tax liability and pay it over to the Revenue Commissioners before the end of June 1991. It must then return its accounts to the Revenue Commissioners by the end of September 1991. If you fail to make your return in time then you face an immediate surcharge of 10% of the amount payable. So if you're due to pay £2,000 by July 1991 but do not return your profits until October 1991 you have to pay £2,200.

Key Dates for Self-Assessment for Companies

1. Accounting Period Ends	2. Due Date for Payment of Tax	3. Filing Date for Return Form CT1
October	April	July
November	May	August
December	June	September
January	July	October
February	August	November
March	September	December
April	October	January
May	November	February
June	December	March
July	January	April
August	February	May
September	March	June

If the company is liable to make returns for Advance Corporation Tax (on Form ACT1) and of Annual Payments (on Form CT2), the dates for filing tax returns and dates for payment of tax on those returns are one month earlier than those specified in column 2 above.

All companies must have an auditor. Most use the same firm of accountants to prepare and submit their accounts to the Revenue Commissioners. There are separate forms for you to fill in when you are sending in your tax and your returns. Make sure you use them to ensure your payments go to the right place in the Revenue Commissioners. One person we know didn't have a form and sent in a cheque and explanatory letter. Unfortunately the letter was never read by the people in Revenue and the cheque was lodged to an unaccountable account and he was charged interest because they thought he hadn't paid.

If you are a sole trader or in a partnership you have to pay your tax on 1st November. Now this is where the end of your accounting period becomes very important. If your year ends on 31 March 1991 you pay tax in November 1990. This isn't such a great idea because you are paying tax in November based on your profits to the end of the following March. If however your tax year ends on 30 April, 1991 you pay tax for that year on 1st November 1991. This puts you in a much better position to calculate your tax bill as you have six months or so after the end of your tax year to do it. So remember, March 1991 is in the 90/91 tax year and April 1991 is in the 91/92 tax year.

Value Added Tax (VAT)

Value Added Tax is payable on most goods and services in the country. If your turnover exceeds £32,000 per annum for goods or £15,000 for services then you need to be registered for VAT. This means you must add VAT on to whatever price you charge your customers. To register for VAT you complete a form from the VAT Administration office (see page 258), return it to the Inspector and you will then be given a VAT number.

You can choose to pay VAT once a year or every two months. If you pay just once a year it does cut down on the administrative hassle which can be helpful. But it also means that you dish out a big lump of money at once. Some find it easier to pay as they go along every two months.

If you're in a service industry particularly you can elect to pay your VAT on a cash receipt basis or on an invoice basis. If you go on a cash receipt basis you pay VAT when you receive the cash, which means you've actually got the cash in at the stage you pay the VAT. If you go for the invoice basis you pay VAT when you raise the invoice and not when you get paid. So if you have a good month and send out £10,000 worth of invoices you end up with a huge VAT bill before you get a penny in. The Revenue Commissioners have a guide to VAT which is available from your local VAT office.

PAYE

Pay As You Earn (PAYE) is a method of collecting income tax on salaries and wages. You as the employer are obliged to deduct tax from your employees and pay it to the Collector General. The Revenue Commissioners have yet another booklet called *Employer's Guide to PAYE* which tells you all about what you need to do and when you need to do it.

PRSI

Pay Related Social Insurance (PRSI) is also deducted by you the employer. PRSI is made up of a number of different components: Social Insurance, Occupational Injury, Redundancy, various levies and a health contribution. The total contribution is made up of an employee's and an employer's share. The contribution is paid to the Collector General of the Revenue Commissioners through the PAYE system. The Department of Social Welfare (see page 254) produce an *Employer's Guide* to the pay-related social insurance contribution system.

PRSI can be a fairly heavy burden on a lot of companies. From time to time there are Government schemes which enable you to take on new employees without having to pay PRSI. So watch out for these schemes.

Do I Need Solicitors and Accountants?

If you are Ms Lone Wolf or a sole trader then it's not absolutely necessary—but it is advisable. Buying or renting a premises, taking on a lease or entering into contracts takes a lot of time and attention to detail. As you will probably be up to your ears anyway getting your company started, having a solicitor to handle leases and the like means you can forget about the small print and let him or her get on with it.

If you plan to enter into a partnership with someone, even if it's your best friend, spouse or lover, it is advisable to have what solicitors call a partnership agreement. Sometimes partnerships work, sometimes they don't. When they don't, life is a lot easier if you have an agreement in place and can get your solicitor to sort out all the bits and pieces to terminate the partnership. It's also useful to know in advance what will happen if one of the partners dies. Will half of what you've put all that blood, sweat and tears into wind up in your deceased partner's estate? Does a spouse have the right to come in and take over half of it? Would you be in a position to buy out the spouse? There is a partnership insurance policy which is funded by the partnership where you can conclude a buy/sell agreement and each partner agrees to effect the policy for the benefit of the surviving partner. One agrees to buy the other person's share and the other agrees that his or her spouse will sell on their death.

If you form a limited company then a solicitor will advise and help you with setting up and registering the company. To do this you need to decide on a name for the company—get approval from the Companies Office to make sure you're not clashing with another already in existence. Define the main objective of the business and decide on the share capital of the company. You can buy a readymade company "off the peg" which will have its own name and constitution documents which are known as memorandum and articles of associates. Either way there is a fair amount of documentation to be processed and procedures to be gone through and solicitors and accountants come in very useful for this.

An accountant should save you more money every year than he or she costs. Whether you choose an accountant working on her own or go for one of the big accountancy firms depends on you and your circumstances. Some feel it's best to develop an ongoing relationship with one individual who can get to know you and your business and whom you can call at any time without each minute spent on the telephone to them costing you an arm and a leg. Others think that the variety of services available from a large company is more beneficial. Whichever route you choose, having an accountant prepare your accounts seems to give you better credibility with the tax people and the banks. Your accountant is obviously putting his reputation on the line but at the same time should be up to date with the latest tax laws to be able to make the most of the tax systems for you and your business.

Insurance

And now we come to the "it'll never happen to me" syndrome. You can hear them: "I'll never get run over by a bus." "Nobody will slip on a wet floor in my shop." "My factory couldn't burn down." Unfortunately these things do happen and you need to be insured in case they happen to you.

There are two categories of insurance—general and life. On the general side there is employer's liability if you are employing people. This means that if one of your employees has an accident while working for you, and they claim against you, then you're covered.

If you have a business where members of the public walk in your door (invited or otherwise) to do business or make enquiries, then you should think about public liability. So if someone comes in to see you and trips over a carpet and breaks their nose you're covered. If you run a cash business then you may need cash-in-transit or cash-on-the-premises type of cover. There are also the burglary, theft and fire areas to think about.

Incidentally, if there is a fire and your factory is burnt to the ground, there is a consequential loss cover which will allow you to relocate and continue to trade until you rebuild your old premises. There is also product liability available whereby, if somebody claims that a fault in your product caused them damage, your insurance covers you.

If you are ill and cannot work life insurance and income continuance are obviously very important, especially if you are the only person in the company. One of the insurance companies recently introduced a scheme which includes life cover, whereby if you become ill with a major illness like heart attack, stroke or cancer, they will pay you a lump sum and allowance while you are in hospital which will not affect your VHI cover.

If the success of your company revolves around one or two key people, there is key person insurance; if that person dies you have money to keep the place ticking over until somebody else comes on board.

Talk to your broker to identify your needs and decide how much you can afford to pay in insurance premiums. A broker has access to all the insurance companies and should be able to get you the best prices.

"Review, review, review," was what one broker said as he remembered the man who bought his house for £5,000 twenty years ago and just continued to pay his premium by standing order. The house is now worth £50,000 but his insurance cover is still only £5,000.

Appendix 2

Useful Addresses

Agricultural Credit
Corporation
ACC House
Upper Hatch Street
Dublin 2
Tel: 01-780644

The Bolton Trust
Pigeon House Road
Ringsend
Dublin 4
Tel: 01-687155

Bord Fáilte
Baggot Street Bridge
Dublin 2
Tel: 01-760871; 616500

Bord lascaigh Mhara
Crofton Road
Dun Laoghaire
Co Dublin
Tel: 01-841544

Business Technology
Centre
IDA Enterprise Centre
North Mall
Cork
Tel: 021-397711

Central Statistics Office
Earlsfort Terrace
Dublin 2
Tel: 01-767531

Confederation of Irish
Industry
Confederation House
Kildare Street
Dublin 2
Tel: 01-779801

Crafts Council of Ireland
Powerscourt Townhouse
Centre
South William Street
Dublin 2
Tel: 01-6797368

CTT
Dublin
Merrion Hall
Strand Road
Sandymount
Dublin 4
Tel: 01-695011
Telex: 93678 CTT EI
FAX: 01-695820

Cork
67/69 South Mall
Cork
Tel: 021-271251/271252
FAX: 021-271347

Limerick
The Granary
Michael Stre
Limerick
Tel: 061-49811/49908
Telex: 70210 CTT EI
FAX: 061-43683

Sligo
Finisklin Industrial Estate
Sligo
Tel: 071-69477/69478
Telex: 38901CTTS EI
FAX: 071- 61896

Waterford
Western Industrial Estate
Cork Road
Waterford
Tel: 051-78577
Telex: 39278 CTTWEII
FAX: 051-79220

Department of Labour
Davitt House
Mespil Road
Dublin 4
Tel: 01-765861

Department of Social
Welfare
PRSI Section
Gandon House
Amiens Street
Dublin
Tel: 01-786444

Dublin Business
Innovation Centre
The Tower Enterprise
Centre
Pearse Street
Dublin 2
Tel: 01-713111

Dublin General PAYE
District
Employers Division
Lyon House
Cathal Brugha Street
Dublin 1
Tel: 01-746821, Extn 18

Eolas: The Irish Science
and Technology Agency
Glasnevin
Dublin 9
Tel: 01-370101

FÁS
Head Office
27-33 Upper Baggot
Street
Dublin 4
Phone 01-685777
Telex: 93313 FAS EI
FAX: 01- 682691

Athlone
Garrycastle
Athlone
Co Westmeath
Tel: 0902-75128/ 74481
FAX: 0902-74795

Baldoyle
Baldoyle Ind Est
Baldoyle
Dublin 13
Tel: 01-391144
Telex: 33410 FAS EI
FAX: 01-391362

Ballyfermot
Ballyfermot Hill
Ballyfermot
Dublin 10
Tel: 01-6266211
Telex: 90776 FAS EI
FAX: 01-6264135

Cabra
Bannow Road
Cabra
Dublin 7
Tel: 01-303133
Telex: 32902 FAS EI
FAX: 01-388788

Centre City Dublin
57-60 Jervis Street
Dublin 1
Tel: 01-726877
Telex: 32903 FAS EI
FAX: 01-726182

**Temporary Training
Centres**

Ballina
"Riverside"
Church Road
Ballina
Co Mayo
Tel: 096-2192
FAX: 096-70608

Cork
Rossa Avenue
Bishopstown
Cork
Tel: 021-544377
Telex: 75156 FAS EI
FAX: 021-544291

Dundalk
Industrial Estate
Coes Road,
Dundalk,
Co Louth
Tel: 042-32311
Telex: 43764 FAS EI
FAX: 042-32117

Finglas
Poppintree Ind. Estate
Jamestown Road
Finglas
DUBLIN 11
Tel: 01-348311
Telex: 30187 FASEI
FAX; 01-346336

Galway
Industrial Estate
Mervue
GALWAY
Tel: 091-51260
Telex: 50198 FAS EI
FAX: 091-53590

Gaoth Dobhair
Na Coire Beaga
Leitir Cheanainn
Co Dhun na nGall
Guthán; 075-31211
Telex:42121 FAS EI
FAX: 075-31114

Letterkenny
Ballyraine Ind. Estate
Ramelton Road
Letterkenny
Tel: 074-22200
FAX: 074-24840

Limerick
Industrial Estate
Raheen
Limerick
Tel: 061-28333
Telex 70252 FAS EI
FAX: 061-301992

Loughlinstown
wyatville Road
Dun Laoghaire
Co Dublin
Tel: 01- 821811
Telex: 91633 EI
FAX: 01-821168

Shannon
Industrial Estate
Shannon
Co Clare
Tel: 061-61133
Telex 72091 FAS EI
FAX: 061-62613

Sligo
Ballytivnan
Sligo
Tel: 071-61121
Telex 40540 FAS EI
FAX: 071-69506

Tallaght
Cookstown Ind. Est
Belgard Road,
Tallaght
Dublin 24
Tel: 01-516411
Telex; 93535 FAS EI
FAX: 01-516021

Tralee
Industrial Estate
Monavalley
Trale,
Co Kerry
Tel: 066-26444
Telex 73142 FAS EI
FAX: 066-23065

Waterford
Industrial Estate
Waterford
Tel: 051-72961/2/3/4/5
Telex 80016 FAS EI
FAX: -051-70896

Wexford
Whitemills North
Industrial Estate
Wexford
Tel: 053-43602
FAX: 053-41718

Galway Business
Innovation Centre
Hines Building
St Augustine Street
Galway
Tel: 091-67974

ICC: Industrial Credit
Corporation
32 Harcourt Street
Dublin 2
Tel: 01-720055

IDA
Dublin Region
Wilton Park House
Wilton Place
Dublin 2
Tel: 01-686633
FAX: 01-605095

East Region
Wilton Park House
Wilton Place
Dublin 2
Tel: 01-686633
FAX: 01-605095

South-East Region
IDA Industrial Estate,
Cork Road, Waterford
Tel: 051-72911
FAX: 051-72719

North-East Region
Finnabair Industrial
Estate
 Dundalk
 Co Louth
Tel: 042-31261/39031
FAX: 042-39034

South-West Region
Industry House
Rossa Avenue
Bishopstown
Co Cork
Tel: 021-343555
FAX: 021-343444

Co Kerry
57 High Street
Killarney
Co Kerry
Tel: 064-34133
FAX: 064-34135

West Region
IDA Industrial Estate
Mervue
Galway
Tel: 091-511111
FAX: 091-51515

Midlands Region
Auburn
Dublin Road
Athlone
Co Westmeath
Tel: 0902-72695
FAX: 0902-74516

North-West Region
Finisklin Industrial Estate
Sligo
Tel: 071-61311
FAX: 071- 61896

Donegal Region
Portland House
Port Road
Letterkenny
Co Donegal
Tel: 074-21155
FAX: 074-21424

Industrial Credit
Corporation PLC
32 Harcourt St
Dublin 2
Tel: 01-720055

Irish Exporters
Association
Marshalsea House
Merchants Quay
Dublin 8
Tel: 01-770285

Irish Franchise
Association Ltd
13 Frankfield Terrace
Summerhill South
Cork
Tel: 021-270859

Irish Goods Council
Merrion Hall
Strand Road
Dublin 4
Tel: 01-696011

Irish Management
Institute
Clonard
Sandyford Rd
Dublin 16
Tel: 01-956911

Irish Quality Association
Merrion Hall
Strand Road
Dublin 4
Tel: 01-695255

Limerick Innovation
Centre
Enterprise House
Plassey Technological
Park
Limerick
Tel: 061-338177

The Marketing Institute
South County Business
Park
Leopardstown
Dublin 18
Tel: 01-952355

Nadcorp
The National
Development Corporation
Ltd
Wilton Park House
Wilton Place
Dublin 2
Tel: 01-600611

Office of the Revenue
Commissioners
Dublin Castle
Dublin 2
Tel: 01-6792777

The Patents Office
45 Merrion Square
Dublin 2
Tel: 01-614144

The Registrar of
Companies
Companies Registration
Office
Dublin Castle
Dublin 2
Tel: 01-614222

Registrar of Friendly
Societies
13 Hume Street
Dublin 2
Tel: 01-614333

Shannon Development
Company
Regional Development
Centre Manager
Clare Business Centre
Francis Street
Ennis
Co Clare

The Small Firms
Association
Confederation House
Kildare Street
Dublin 2
Tel: 01-779801

Teagasc
Agriculture and Food
Development Authority
19 Sandymount Avenue
Ballsbridge
Dublin4
Tel: 01-688188

Udarás na Gaeltachta
3ú Urlá
Teach IPC
35 Bothar Siolbhroin
Droichead na Dothr,
Baile Átha Cliath 4
Teileafón: 01- 607888
Teileacs: 93655
FAX: 01-686030

Na Forbacha
Gaillimh
Teileafón; 091-92011
Teileacs: 50159
FAX: 091-92037

An Bun Beag
Co Dhun na nGall
Teileafón: 075-31200
FAX: 075-31319

An Daingean
Co Chiarrai
Teileafón: 066-51658

Beal an Mhuirthid,
Co Mhaigh Eo.
Teileafón: 097-81418

VAT Administration Office
Castle House
South Great Georges
Street
Dublin 2
Tel: 01-6792777

Voluntary Health
InsuranceBoard
VHI House
Lower Abbey Street
Dublin 1
Tel: 01-724499

Index